"The clinical wisdom and insights of Barnard, one of the most skillful and thorough child psychologists and clinicians I have known, shine throughout this book. Parents who read this book will understand what childhood depression is, how it is diagnosed, how it is treated, and what they can do to advocate for their child. This book has my enthusiastic endorsement for its balance of clinical wisdom and research-based recommendations. Parents and clinicians working with depressed children will find this book a most useful resource."

    —Michael A. Rapoff, Ph.D., professor, Behavioral
        Sciences Department of Pediatrics, University
        of Kansas Medical Center

Helping Your Depressed Child

A STEP-BY-STEP GUIDE FOR PARENTS

Martha Underwood Barnard, Ph.D.

NEW HARBINGER PUBLICATIONS, INC.

Publisher's Note

This publication is designed to provide accurate and authoritative information in regard to the subject matter covered. It is sold with the understanding that the publisher is not engaged in rendering psychological, financial, legal, or other professional services. If expert assistance or counseling is needed, the services of a competent professional should be sought.

Distributed in the U.S.A. by Publishers Group West; in Canada by Raincoat Books; in Great Britain by Hi Marketing, Ltd.; in South Africa by Real Books, Ltd.; in Australia by Boobook; and in New Zealand by Tandem Press.

Copyright © 2003 by Martha Underwood Barnard
New Harbinger Publications, Inc.
5674 Shattuck Avenue
Oakland, CA 94609

Cover design by Poulson and Gluck
Text design by Tracy Marie Carlson

ISBN 1-57224-322-8 Paperback
All Rights Reserved

Printed in the United States of America

New Harbinger Publications' Web site address: www.newharbinger.com

05   04   03
10   9   8   7   6   5   4   3   2   1
First printing

This book is dedicated to:

My husband, Howard

My daughters, Mandye and Beckye

My parents, Johnson and Wilhelmine Lingelbach Underwood

My siblings, Mary Ann, Jack, and Katye

My in-laws, Tony, Ann, and Jim

My nephews and nieces

My aunts and uncles

My cousins

My wonderful friends

My colleagues and students

Contents

Introduction

☙ *Kim's Story*

Kim's parents were increasingly concerned over their beautiful blond daughter. Her eyes looked so dull. She had always been a very good student and very social. If there were a party going on, Kim would be there. Other children had always wanted her to play with them because she was so much fun. Only a year ago, she was given the award for the most enthusiastic soccer player. Now these aspects of Kim's life had changed dramatically.

Kim's parents received a call from her teacher who said that Kim just didn't seem as interested in school as she used to. She was forgetting to hand in assignments. Her work was sloppy, and when she did her work, it was done incorrectly. Her grades had dropped from Bs and As to Ds and an occasional C. She told her parents that school was boring.

Her parents felt Kim seemed so sad. She was not participating in social activities as much anymore. If she was invited to go to her friend's house, she would make up an excuse so that she didn't have to go. She told her mother that her friends just weren't any fun anymore. Her mother and her teachers noticed that when she was with friends she was extremely irritable. It seemed that her peers did not want to be around her like they had in the past.

Life at home had changed, too. Kim seemed to sleep much of the afternoons and much of her days during the weekends. What puzzled her parents is that they would hear her wake up at least two times each night. When they got up in the morning they would find Kim up, staring at the television. Now, she regularly woke up at 5:30 A.M. and couldn't go back to sleep.

Mealtimes became a major source of conflict between Kim and her father. He felt she ate far too much. He was amazed that at some meals she ate more than he did. Her once-small figure was now beginning to look plump, and they could not keep food in their house. They figured she must be sick and took her to the doctor.

Does Kim's behavior sound anything like that of your own child? If your child shows signs of sadness, irritability, a change in grades, increased fatigue, and a change in weight, then they may need help with childhood depression.

ξΟ

Two and one half per cent of all school-age children are identified as having depression and yet the majority of books, articles, and classes on the subject address the problem in relation to the adolescent population. Rarely do these sources deal with depression and the school-age child. More importantly, the risk of suicide is rarely thought about for the school-age child. However, as recently as 1997, "suicide was the third leading cause of death in 10- to 24-year olds" (National Institute of Mental Health 2002).

Prevalence increases with age and rises to 6 percent at puberty. Boys and girls experience it at an equal rate during prepuberty, with an increase to a higher incidence among girls at puberty, resulting in a two-to-one female-to-male ratio (Jellinek and Snyder 1998). Similar to all ages, children have a 70 percent recurrence rate after five years of the initial onset of their symptoms (Barton 2001). Therefore, it seems to behoove parents of children with or without depression to get appropriate help for their child as soon as there are signs of depression or life situations that would set the child up for depression. Hopefully, preventative measures would decrease the impact of the child's depression and reduce the consequences of the effects of the symptoms. Taking early action may also make a recurrence of a depressive episode for your child less likely.

The History of Childhood Depression

Depression has only recently been recognized in the health care community as a possible diagnosis for children. Before that, it was thought that depression was only an illness of adolescents and adults. The incidence has increased significantly over the last fifty years for a variety of reasons, some of which we can identify and others that are still under investigation.

Prior to the 1970s, it was believed that depression was a reaction to the loss of a loved one. Freud described similarities in the reaction to the loss of a loved one and "melancholia," his word for depression (Jellinek and Snyder 1998). These reactions included sadness, changes in eating and sleeping, and a loss of interest of things going on in the outside world (Jellinek and Snyder 1998). Melancholia was thought to only occur in an individual who had achieved the developmental stages of adolescence or adulthood because this was when the individual had grown to the point to be able to feel guilt. Guilt came as a result of the person having a conscience or, as psychoanalysts put it, a "superego." It was believed that children didn't yet have a conscience, thus this would make them unable to feel guilt and therefore unable to have depression.

In the 1960s others described children as having hidden depression. In other words, children had depression but exhibited it by behaviors such as *encopresis* (fecal soiling) and hyperactivity (Glaser 1968). By the mid-1970s researchers began to report that children had the same depressive symptoms as adolescents and adults, but they expressed them according to their different developmental abilities. Today it is clearly recognized that children can and do become depressed and that parents are the key individuals to recognize when their child becomes depressed. After all, parents usually know their child better than anyone.

How This Book Can Help

While *Helping Your Depressed Child* cannot take the place of a therapist helping your child through their depression, it can be a valuable resource guide for you and your child during this difficult time. You will also find it helpful when you're not sure when and if to seek help and exactly what type of help your child might need in the first place. Parents often have questions regarding symptoms, their cause, and exactly what might be done to answer those questions. This book will help to answer these and other questions that surround serious life events that may have the potential for causing depression in your child. It will also offer you powerful techniques to help your child through this rough time. You may even find that the information and techniques in this book will not only help you with your child but can also help you with your own down times. A parent that is well and coping with the stressors in their life is more likely to be able to help their child with their illness.

Another reason for this book is to provide an answer to Surgeon General David Satcher's request for preventive interventions to help reduce the impact of risk factors on the vulnerable child. Specifically, the request was for parent-education programs and education programs for children that would help depressed kids cope. Satcher stressed the importance of families being "essential partners in the delivery of mental health services for their children" (U.S.D.H.H.S 1999). To make you a partner with mental-health professionals you must learn first what childhood depression is, and then how to be an advocate for your child in the health care system. Finally, it would help tremendously if you knew actual psychological strategies and techniques to help your child cope with some of the things that are causing the depression. Coping with a mental illness requires teamwork, an effective treatment, a strong parent advocate, and age-appropriate cognitive behavioral interventions. This book will help you accomplish all of these goals.

An Ounce of Prevention

Although this book has been written specifically to help depressed children and their parents, it would be a valuable tool in helping prevent depression in any child. The strategies and information I'm offering will assist any parent who is worried about a child who seems to be struggling. The interventions in *Helping Your Depressed Child*, including developing strong parent advocacy and good discipline programs and using cognitive behavioral therapy, can aid any child who is in need of a bit of extra help.

If the call is for depression prevention, then it is time to know if your child is showing any early warning signs that depression is a high possibility. If the red flags are there then it is important that the adults close to these at-risk children know what to do to prevent the child from having more serious emotional consequences or a suicide later.

Where We're Going

As you read, I hope to begin helping you learn about how to address the wide range of problems that arise for parents when taking care of a child with depression or for a child facing life circumstances that have the high potential to set off depression. You'll start in chapters 1 and 2 by gaining a comprehensive understanding of what depression is, its causes, and the multiple types of depression. Also in chapter 2, I will help you become acquainted with the importance of the medical history and its ultimate relationship to the accurate diagnosis made from your child's symptoms. In this same chapter, I'll guide you on selecting your doctors. Chapter 3 will cover the different causes thought to be responsible for childhood depression. In chapter 4, I will present a variety of interventions for the child with depression, including a suicide-prevention contract. We'll also examine the problems confronting children in school, including teasing and learning disabilities. I will make suggestions for interventions for both of these problems. Additionally, I will present information on common-sense discipline, including the use of behavioral strategies, in chapter 5. Following this, in chapter 6 you'll learn techniques to help, such as cognitive behavioral interventions, relaxation techniques, social-skills training, and nutritional concerns. These techniques can help your child learn to think more positively and improve their self-esteem. But there are times when the diagnosis just doesn't seem to fit, and chapter 7 will help you with these times, as I present some of the alternative diagnoses your doctor might consider. Chapter 8 will include material on selected antidepressant medications and their actions, dosages, and side effects. I hope this will help you in the event your child is placed on a medication so that you will be aware of the actions of the medications as they relate to your child's illness and their unique response to a pharmacological intervention. In chapter 9, I will look at loss in children's lives. These losses will include the loss of a loved one and or the loss experienced when parents get divorced. After these more detailed chapters, I will present a comprehensive summary in chapter 10.

Summary

In my work as a nurse and therapist for troubled kids, I've had more than thirty years to see the importance of parents' and other caring adults' proactive stands in helping children cope with life circumstances. It's this work in my clinical practice that inspired me to bring this information to you, the parents of children who are sad and struggling in their everyday lives. I hope this book serves as a resource, whether you and your child are in or out of therapy. A well-informed parent is equipped with the necessary information and techniques to advocate for their child in the best and the worst of circumstances.

As for the young girl who started this chapter, Kim's parents took her for an evaluation with their family doctor, who then referred them to a mental-health professional. She was diagnosed with depression and treated with both therapy and medication. Within a few weeks Kim began to act like her old self. Her parents were amazed that a school-aged child could suffer from depression. They had always believed this was a condition of adults. Now they know how to listen to and assist a child who is calling out for help. Is your child calling to you?

Chapter 1

Defining Childhood Depression

✍ Danny's Story

I looked into the eyes of Danny, the young, innocent boy sitting before me. They were cold and expressionless. Dark circles appeared under each eye, screaming out that this small body and young mind were suffering from the fatigue and exhaustion characteristic of depression. How could anyone so young and innocent be so sad? The parents sat next to their child, one on each side. They were obviously frightened and concerned. They feared that their child suffered from some major physical illness, perhaps leukemia.

When Danny's parents first learned that their child was falling asleep in class and that his grades and behavior had changed significantly, they grounded him. But this action did not seem to make any difference in his school behaviors. He continued to fail in his class work and to act out. After being at their wits end, his parents decided to seek professional advice, so they took Danny to his primary medical doctor. A thorough physical was conducted and lab tests were done. The doctor said everything was normal. He advised the parents, "Take Danny home, and make sure he gets plenty of rest. It's probably the flu." After a week nothing had changed, but Danny returned to school anyway. He was still drained of energy and began complaining of severe headaches. The school nurse let Danny's parents know that he was in the nurse's office frequently with a variety of other physical complaints such as stomachaches and leg aches. She described him as very sad and tearful. She asked Danny's parents to take him back to his doctor for further evaluation.

The doctor did another physical and further blood tests and again the results were normal. The doctor noticed that Danny seemed very sad and very fatigued. The child reminded him of an adult with depression, but the doctor doubted that this was what this child had. After all, he had never heard of children experiencing depression. In spite of his uncertainty, he decided to refer the child to me to see what my impression was. After a thorough history and psychological evaluation, I determined the diagnosis to be depression.

℘

A Parent's Concern

This story has been and still is all-too-common. You are reading this book because you most likely have a similar concern about your child or a child well known to you. For reasons that are not understood, adults still underestimate the possibility of depression in children. They look for other reasons, even outlandish ones, for a child's sad, irritable, and nonachieving behavior. All too often it is a child's threat of running away or killing themselves that finally gets the attention of adults in their environment. Unfortunately, sometimes it takes a suicide attempt or the successful completion of that attempt to finally convince the child's loved ones and other significant adults in their lives that depression is a reality for some children. Depression is painful for the child and their family, and it must be treated before it results in a tragedy.

You probably are reading this book because you're a good parent and you have concerns about your child. It may be a very scary time for you. Parents don't like to see their children sad. You probably find yourself staying awake at night, worrying about your child. You may even cry or obsess over whether your child is just having a mood swing or whether there is something really wrong.

When your son or daughter comes home from school perhaps you bombard them with questions of how their day was and how they feel. You also question them about whom they sat next to at lunch and whom they played with on the playground. You notice that kids are not calling your child as much as earlier in the school year. It seems like they're being left out of the birthday parties and the sleepovers. You sense that with each question you ask, your child seems to withdraw from you a little more. What's going on? You are heartsick.

A school progress report arrives with the news that your child has not been handing in their homework—but they have told you repeatedly that they have no homework. Now they are making Ds and Fs. You're angry with the teacher. Why hasn't she called you? Surely she can motivate them better to get their work done. You feel she is giving them too much homework. Maybe she's not a good teacher. Your child's father is angry because his child should be doing better in school. He screams, "Why can't you make them do their work?" Your other children begin to ask questions about what is wrong with their brother or sister. Your marriage becomes strained.

Now you are trying to identify what you have done to make them different from their peers. Your thoughts surge ahead to their adolescence. You become quite anxious and think, "They will become one of these teenagers who quits school and uses drugs." The more you worry, the more hopeless the situation seems. After all, look at all the troubled teenagers out there. This must be the way they start. Now your family is faced with that same future. Where do you go for help?

A Response

It's true that most of the things parents worry about *could* happen. However, what interests me is that many parents become so concerned about what is going to happen to their children when they become teenagers that they forget what is happening to them as children. These parents' current responsibilities don't hold their attention when compared to the dramatic future scenarios they picture in their minds. But it's important to pay attention to the present day. Children need to be understood. The only way to help safeguard your child's future is to determine what is going on with your child now and then do something about it. You'll find that it feels much better to take action than to worry about what might happen someday. If your child sees you take action they are more likely to take action for themselves. Your child will respond to their illness as you respond to their illness.

Defining Mood Disorders

Danny's story presents some of the problems parents are faced with when their child begins exhibiting signs and symptoms of depression. First of all, very often the schoolteacher believes that the child is just not trying or is disrespectful. School nurses are faced with numerous physical complaints from children that feel sad. In fact, these nurses are often the ones that refer the child to their physician to have a physical to determine if there is any physical illness present. This is a wise move and a necessary one, since so many of the physical symptoms of depression look like other serious physical illnesses.

Many times the physician is impressed with how sick your child may look but may be unaware that your child can be depressed. Thus there are often numerous tests done and repeated to rule out serious physical illnesses only to find out that they continue to come out normal. It's a relief to get normal test results, but then what is wrong with your child?

Unfortunately health professionals often do not realize that school-age children can get depressed and thus frequently miss an opportunity for early intervention. In this section you'll become familiar with the different types of mood disorders and the signs of possible suicide so that even if your doctor misses it the first time, you can intervene.

I have lots of parents, and in some cases even children, ask how psychiatry and psychology determine a diagnosis. Before we discuss the actual process for diagnosing, I want to define the different types of depression. These definitions can be found in a text entitled the *Diagnostic and Statistical Manual of Mental Disorders*, often referred to as the *DSM-IV-TR* (American Psychiatric Association 2000). I don't suggest that you go out and buy this book. However, in the event you want to use it or purchase it as a resource, it can be found in most bookstores and, of course, libraries.

You may have noticed that earlier I used the term "mood disorders." Here's what I mean by that. *Mood disorders* are a group of disorders that are characterized as affecting the physical, thought, perceptual, and social processes of an individual (Weiten 1997). There are two types of mood disorders affecting people. They are *unipolar*, where the mood is on the depressed end of a mood continuum, and *bipolar* where the mood is on both ends of a mood continuum (Weiten 1997). In this latter case, the moods would range from depressed moods to manic moods (unusually high energy, feelings of grandiosity, and so forth). The *DSM-IV-TR* provides a list of diagnostic criteria that are used to define the specific type of mood disorder. The criteria used for adults are also used for children and adolescents, with some exceptions. These criteria are discussed in chapter 2.

Think of a straight line labeled "mood continuum." On the left end of that line are the unipolar disorders, or those associated with a decrease in energy and motivation along with distorted perceptions and thoughts and a lack of social skills. The other end of the line represents an abundance of energy and excitation known as mania. As I mentioned earlier, unipolar includes one end of this continuum and bipolar includes both ends of this continuum. For the purpose of this book, depression will be the major focus of discussion. However, one cannot be evaluated for depression without having bipolar depression considered.

Depression

Depression, also sometimes called a "major depressive episode," is when your child experiences a depressed mood, hopelessness, and loss of pleasure in normal childhood activities. This lasts at least two weeks and throughout most of each day during that time. Your child may exhibit irritability and oppositional behavior with sadness or (unlike adults) without sadness. This does not include sadness or irritability due to bereavement (such as due to the loss of loved one), a medical condition (like poorly controlled diabetes), medications (such as during steroid therapy), substance abuse, schizophrenia, delusional disorders, or other psychotic disorders. We'll get even more specific in chapter 2.

There are other conditions that are associated with depression. The more common ones are believed to be anxiety disorders, dysthymia, conduct disorders, and a substance abuse disorder. Generally speaking, depression occurs after the associated disorders have occurred in a child or adolescent. The exception to this is when substance abuse is present (Biederman et al. 1995; U.S.D.H.H.S. 1999). However, it's important to keep in mind that if your child is depressed they may be attracted to alcohol and substances for the purpose of treating themselves for their feelings of hopelessness and sadness.

In other situations, depression and another mental disorder may not occur as a result of each other but occur as two independent entities. For example, depression and a conduct disorder may occur separately. This is thought to be due to the child's or adolescent's response to inadequate parenting (U.S.D.H.H.S. 1999).

Dysthymia

Dysthymia is a chronic, milder form of a mood disorder like depression. If your child has dysthymia, they may seem to always be in a bad mood or to have a "chip on their shoulder," which results in a difficult adjustment in their life. It usually lasts for at least an average of four years and during that time, occurs throughout most days (U.S.D.H.H.S. 1999). Although it may seem milder, it can result in a more major depression or may occur at the same time, and is referred in this report as "double depression." Like depression, dysthymia can end in suicide if it is not adequately treated.

Bipolar Disorder

Bipolar disorder (manic depression) is a form of a mixed depressive disorder as I described earlier in this chapter. If you can picture the mood continuum, you will recall that bipolar includes both ends of the continuum. So the depressive symptoms and manic symptoms are mixed. This disorder presents with (or shows symptoms of) an abnormal elevated or irritable mood lasting at least one week, and it may require hospitalization. It has been only recently that bipolar disorder was diagnosed in children. Research is being conducted at numerous mental-health sites to help you and your health professionals understand this disorder as it pertains to children and adolescents.

There are risk factors for developing bipolar disorder at a later age. They are

* Diagnosis of depression during childhood

* Psychotic symptoms (like hallucinations) at the time of the first diagnosis

* A family history of bipolar disorder

* Mania when first treated with an antidepressant medication

There are a number of other disorders that have to be considered when your child presents with what looks like depression. They include physical illnesses, medication side effects, substance abuse, psychosis (hallucinations), adjustment reactions, attention deficit hyperactivity disorder (ADHD), anxiety, depression with a seasonal pattern (depression during cloudy seasons or certain times of the year such as the beginning of school), post-traumatic stress disorder (disorder after trauma), oppositional defiant disorder (strong-willed), low self-esteem, and bereavement. You should remember that when these conditions are seen in a child, there are also other associated problems within the child's family context that must be assessed. These include parental mood disorders and anxiety disorders, siblings' behavioral and emotional problems, and poor parenting skills. This book's major focus will be childhood depression; however, there will be other conditions discussed throughout the book and specifically in chapters 7 and 8.

Adjustment Disorders

Adjustment disorder with depressive symptoms is just what it sounds like: it is your child's response to some negative event to which they react with sadness that seems to be more than what would have been expected for others in a similar situation. Such children may have trouble in school or socially. Usually this does not last a long time, but it can last for several months. If the sadness doesn't lift when things change for the better in the child's life, then a professional needs to evaluate your child.

Suicidal Behavior

Suicide is a real problem for children and adolescents. It is a myth that a child can be too young to commit suicide, and talk about suicide should always be taken seriously. The incidence for suicide attempts peaks during the midadolescent years and mortality increases throughout adolescence, making it the third leading cause of death for this age group (U.S.D.H.H.S. 1999).

Depression is the major risk factor for committing suicide for both children and adolescents. Suicide in the family and prior suicide attempts are considered important indicators of potential suicide. Other risk factors are peers committing suicide and celebrities committing suicide. As strange as this may sound, it's thought to be due to children and adolescents thinking that if these other people thought it was a good way to deal with problems, then it's probably okay for the child, too. Also, watch your child for signs that they're thinking about suicide if they are in a social conflict with friends, has been diagnosed with a serious illness, has a dysfunctional family, or has had a close friend, parent, sibling, or relative just die. These signs include talk with phrases such as "wanting to die," "being better off dead," "kill myself," "commit suicide," and are all warning signs of possible suicide. Notes or drawings with themes or content related to death need to be considered big red flags. Additionally, if your child is suddenly giving away valued personal possessions, consider that a cry for help.

Homes with firearms are environments that place children at risk for attempting suicide. Weapons should always be removed from the home if a child or family member is depressed. In all homes, firearms and knives should always be locked up. Additionally, prescribed or over-the-counter medications need to be locked up along with other toxic substances in the home.

Finally, one more word of caution: just because your child has not had a history of depression does not make them immune from trying to commit suicide in the event a crisis occurs in their life. I worry about this especially in children who have diagnoses such as attention deficit hyperactivity disorder (ADHD). Children with this diagnosis may have impulsivity as one of their major symptoms. In other words, they do things without considering the consequences. All children with impulsivity, whether diagnosed with ADHD or not, have a high risk for doing things that may harm themselves or others. In this case, they may attempt suicide without thinking about the true consequences. Additionally, school-age children don't believe they are mortal. So when they attempt suicide it may be more as a cry for help than as a way to end their life.

Summary

In this first chapter we've learned about Danny and the common frustration that parents face when seeking professional help for their child. All too often teachers see your child as lazy, bored, or lacking the capabilities for achieving at their grade level. Additionally, your child spends time in the principal's office because of behavior problems or rudeness toward faculty and peers— expressions of depression. The nurse's office also becomes a frequent stop for your child because of their myriad physical complaints. The nurse is usually impressed with the physical and mood changes of your child and refers them to your family physician for an evaluation to rule out a physical illness. Rarely is a physical illness found, and after frequent physical checks and numerous laboratory tests your child is sent to a mental-health professional to be evaluated for an emotional diagnosis. You've learned the basic diagnoses that may result from this doctor's visit, and which will be the theme of this book. Finally, I've tried to stress that you must *always* believe a child when they talk about suicide.

In the next chapter the focus will be on the specifics of making the diagnosis. We'll look at the criteria for making a diagnosis of depression and the importance of the parent's role when providing information to health professionals and mental-health professionals during the diagnostic process. You will also come to understand the measures and criteria that are frequently used to support the diagnosis of depression.

Chapter 2

What Is Wrong with My Child?

ஒ *Becky's Story*

The teacher has called to discuss Becky's grades with you. She is not get-
ting her schoolwork done and for the past two weeks she has not been
handing in her homework assignments. Becky has been telling you she
has no homework. The teacher reports Becky's grades have not been as
good as in the prior quarter. She is making Cs and Ds when she has
always made As and Bs. You wish she had called you earlier so you
could have been on top of Becky's school problems. You feel embarrassed.
You worry that her teacher thinks you're not a very good parent. The
teacher also tells you that lately Becky has become more of a loner. She
would rather stay inside at recess. Becky stands alone on the playground
and does not participate in the playground games. The teacher tells you
she doesn't seem to have any friends. Your heart feels very heavy and
you feel like crying. A panic feeling comes over you. Why don't the other
kids like her? Every parent wants their kids to be accepted by other kids.
It doesn't seem like anyone ever calls. Becky is not invited to anyone's
house anymore. She acts like she doesn't even know she is left out of
other classmates' parties and sleepovers. If you know, she must know.
You hear the other kids talk about her during carpool. You wonder
"Whom can I confide in? Who can I talk with to see if Becky has a serious
problem?" You wonder if you are just being an over-protective parent.

You consider the teacher to be very knowledgeable about your
child. She has talked to the school counselor and they both agree Becky
needs to be evaluated by a mental-health professional. You feel she needs
an expert to help her.

ஒ

The truth of the matter is, you are the expert on your child. You know and understand your child better than most adults who are involved with her. However, you and your child may need a child specialist in education, nursing, medicine, or psychology to give you an objective opinion on how to help your child and to support both of you.

The problem is that you, like many parents, may bury your head in the sand when it comes to the possibility of anything emotional being wrong with your child. It may be that you're denying something is wrong because of the nature of the ailment. It may be that you have so many other things going on in your personal or family life that you don't have the energy or vigilance to recognize that your child is in emotional pain. However, it is important to take action now.

Getting a Diagnosis

In spite of all the advances in mental-health research and treatment, people are still embarrassed about having a mental-health problem. So often the children in our society are overlooked when it comes to getting help for their emotional problems. I'm not sure why this continues to be a problem, but what I do know is we all have to take steps to change these attitudes. Earlier interventions for these disorders will lead to a better prognosis. Childhood depression is an example of a disorder that needs to be identified early in its course.

Depression may be difficult to diagnose because it is elusive. According to Hafen et al. (1996), it can be understood in a number of ways, including:

- a normal human response to a lifetime event

- a symptom of a medical illness

- a side effect of a treatment for a medical illness

- a syndrome in which there is a neurochemical imbalance

- a combination of all four of these causes

Because of this elusiveness, you may need different types of professional evaluations to be conducted in order to get an accurate diagnosis and determine the cause so that appropriate treatment can be started. There are times when the actual cause cannot be determined, but the child still has symptoms of depression. No matter what the actual diagnosis is, you and your child still need support and guidance.

How to Start

Your child needs to see their medical doctor or nurse practitioner initially to rule out physical ailments that can have symptoms similar to depression. There are a number of medical diagnoses that go along with depressive symptoms. For example, mononucleosis is known to sometimes precede depression or may actually be seen with it. Hypothyroidism is another example of a problem that may result in depressive symptoms.

Also, there are children who have physical complaints that have no medical basis to them. Stomachaches, chest pain, and headaches are just a few of these physical complaints. In the event that no organic reason can be found to explain the physical complaints, it doesn't mean that the child is making them up and that they're not real. They are real to your child. In fact, unexplained physical symptoms are thought to be common in depressed children. These children have a decrease in the neurochemicals serotonin, dopamine, and endorphins in the brain. The decrease of these neurochemicals results in fatigue and an increase in pain, two common symptoms found in children with depression.

It's important to remember that, even if there is nothing found by the medical tests, it doesn't mean that something won't surface later. That is why it is important to have your child thoroughly evaluated by your family doctor or nurse practitioner so that these practitioners can be involved in ongoing evaluation and care of your child. If your doctor cannot find a physical cause for your child's depressive symptoms, then ask the doctor to refer you to a psychologist, social worker, or counselor that they would recommend for an evaluation. It's important that even after your child moves on to one of these new practitioners, your doctor or nurse practitioner maintains close contact with the therapist so that they can share information they have gathered about your child. It will also give them a chance to share their thoughts regarding your child's condition.

Seeing a Mental-Health Professional

Since you are the expert on your child, you will want to bring to the mental-health professional a very detailed history regarding what has been going on in your child's recent life, as well as over their past lifetime. The present and significant past historical information may help your mental-health professional make a more accurate diagnosis. (We'll look at this more closely later in this chapter.)

DSM-IV Criteria

As you recall, I introduced the *DSM-IV-TR* to you as the resource that mental-health professionals use when making the clinical diagnosis of depression. Let's look at the criteria that they use to determine whether your child is depressed. This will give you an idea of what you need to be looking for with your child.

The following are the criteria for depression and are adapted from the *DSM-IV-TR* (2000).

1. The child has a depressed mood, which will occur nearly every day and throughout each day. This depressed mood might be an irritable mood in children. People in the child's environment can observe it in the child or it can be reported by the child.

2. The child has a marked decrease in interest or pleasure in all of their activities. This occurs throughout the entire day and usually most days.

3. The child has significant weight loss or weight gain due to an increase or decrease in the child's appetite. The growth grid kept by your health professional will be the best indicator of the degree of your child's weight change in relation to their height and any changes that are beyond normal for their age. It will also show the trend for their weight.

4. The child's sleep patterns change, resulting in an increase in sleep or insomnia.

5. The child is restless or may have "psychomotor retardation." It can be observed in a variety of settings, and occurs throughout the day.

6. The child is fatigued most days.

7. The child has feelings of worthlessness and a significant amount of inappropriate guilt.

8. The child is not able to think or concentrate, leading to indecisiveness during most days.

9. The child will report recurrent thoughts of death, suicidal ideation (thoughts) without or with a plan for committing suicide, or will actually attempt to commit suicide.

For a diagnosis of depression, your child must have at least five of the nine criteria, and these changes will need to have been present for the same two weeks, not accounted for by other reasons such as a medication, substance abuse, medical illness, or bereavement. The list of the *DSM-IV-TR* criteria should only be used as a guideline and in no way should limit what you report to the doctor or mental-health professional. Even if you're not sure if your child fulfills five of the nine criteria, you might want to talk to a mental-health professional to get their advice and thoughts regarding your concerns and their observations of your child.

Remember again that *you* are the expert. Not one thing that you share with your professionals or one question you ask is stupid. The only stupid question or information is that not asked or shared. If the professional you share it with makes you feel that a piece of information is insignificant or that it was silly of you to ask a particular question, then check it out with that professional. They cannot read your mind and you can't read theirs. You may have misperceived how they were reacting to your concerns and questions. If you still feel they are minimizing your concerns, then you might need to consult a different professional.

Types of Information to Report

The *patient history* (the story of the child's life) in the evaluation process for physical or emotional problems is considered the key for making a diagnosis. It is considered by some as the most important aspect of assessment, and if it is not thorough enough it may result in an inaccurate diagnosis. In the case when your child is not feeling well, you are the holder of that key. You possess the information that enables professionals to begin putting together the puzzle to determine your child's diagnosis. The professional collects this information through an interview using an organized format. If certain pieces of information are not provided or are withheld, it may result in an inaccurate diagnosis or the wrong treatment. This is where your expertise on your child is very helpful to the health professional. The following are some of the key pieces of information you should consider while sharing with the professional voluntarily or while responding to interview questions. Remember that if you fabricate an answer or don't share important information then this might lead to an incorrect diagnosis. This will not help your child.

First, Cut to the Chase

Try saying in one sentence the major thing that concerns you about your child and what your greatest fear is regarding what may happen. This gets out what is concerning you so that the therapist knows right away what you're worried about. If you delay and beat around the bush because you're feeling nervous or silly about being there, you will be doing a disservice to your child. Therapists organize some of their thoughts and questions according to what you tell them in the beginning. They will eventually get to what is really the problem but it will take longer; wouldn't it be easier to start off with your most important concerns?

Providing General Information

In addition to your major concern (known as the "chief complaint" by some professionals), there is important information surrounding that concern that the therapist needs to know. This information and your chief concern will begin to paint a picture of what is going on with your child.

The following is a list that can help you organize your thoughts and information. It's not an exhaustive list and doesn't mean that your child has to have all of these behaviors. They may have some and not the others. Use this list as a way of stimulating you to think about the types of information that should be shared.

- **Change in mood:** irritability; aggressiveness; tearfulness; loss of interest in daily activities; mood swings; fears;

decrease in concentration; guilt; withdrawal from family and friends; low self-esteem

* **Change in behavior:** fidgetiness; slower in accomplishing things; lying; stealing; bullying others; temper tantrums; habits such as nail biting or chewing on clothes; tics; boredom; change in normal activities; self-mutilation; noncompliance with commands; requires multiple reminders; stays in their room most of the time; excessive masturbation

* **Change in eating:** increase in appetite; decrease in appetite; increased weight; decreased weight; feels they are fat; change in behaviors surrounding mealtimes

* **Change in sleeping:** hard time getting to sleep; frequently awakens throughout the night; nightmares; begins sleepwalking; early morning awakenings; hard to awaken in the morning; insomnia; frequent naps; begins sleeping in parent's bed

* **Change in elimination patterns:** new onset of bed-wetting (enuresis); daytime wetting; new onset of fecal soiling; constipation; diarrhea

* **Change in school behavior:** increased absences; resistance to going to school; increased tardiness; noncompliance with the school rules; doesn't like teacher; fails to hand in homework; refuses to do school work; decrease in grades; falling asleep in school; increased physical complaints; more trips to the nurse's office; a target of teasing; victim of bullies; bullies classmates; no best friend; left out of social functions, such as classmates' parties

* **Change in health:** increase in health problems; chronic illness; headaches; stomachaches; chest pain; dizziness; joint aches; urinary tract infections; takes prescribed medication; takes excessive over-the-counter medications (like analgesics); auditory hallucinations

* **Change in the family:** parental fighting; separation; divorce; new marriage; new sibling; sibling with behavior problems; family member with a new, serious medical diagnosis; family member with a chronic illness; family member diagnosed or hospitalized for mental-

health problems; death of a family member; parental loss of employment; family financial loss

* **Other:** best friend moves away; classmate diagnosed with serious illness; classmate in an accident; classmate commits suicide; classmate dies; teacher changes; teacher becomes ill; teacher dies

Prenatal, Delivery, and Newborn

The prenatal, delivery, and newborn history of a child is also very important for your professional to be aware of. If your child is a product of a difficult pregnancy, a difficult delivery or a stormy newborn period, they may end up being special to you in some way. Sometimes this takes the form of the child being over-protected and other times it might be that the child is neglected more than their siblings. Discipline may be lacking or the opposite, very strict. These dynamics may result in the child feeling like they are different from their siblings; or if they don't have siblings, they may feel different from their peers. This could be a set-up for self-esteem problems, thus possibly making the child vulnerable to depression.

This is not to say that these pregnancy, newborn, or early infancy problems always lead to depression. Your child may grow up and be very healthy. I only want to stress to you not to omit or hide this information. It will help your mental-health professional have all the facts, not only to make a diagnosis, but also to help and understand you as a parent. It is essential for your therapist to understand you as a parent and what prenatal, newborn, and infancy events influenced you to be the parent you are. To understand the parents is to understand their child.

* **Prenatal history:** wanted or unwanted pregnancy; replacement baby (replaces a deceased sibling); history of miscarriage; pregnant after infertility; pregnancy complication; severe nausea; prenatal bleeding; premature labor; required bed rest during pregnancy; single mother; marital problems; marital abuse; separation or divorce during pregnancy; alcohol or substance abuse; mental illness; serious accident; acute or chronic illness requiring multiple medications; lack of social support

* **Labor and delivery:** premature labor; long and difficult labor; painful labor and delivery; C-section; low Apgar scores (score of newborn status at the time of birth); premature delivery; multiple newborns

* **Newborn:** sick newborn; jaundiced newborn; colicky newborn; premature newborn requiring long hospitalization; numerous medical procedures; apnea monitor; did not like to be held; multiple births; postpartum depression; breast or bottle fed; suck reflex

Developmental History

The developmental history should be shared as accurately as you can. This is true even if you cannot remember the chronological details regarding language development or when your child began to walk. The thing I have always noted when talking to parents in my practice is that they always remember if something about the development did not seem right to them.

The following are the milestones to be aware of, if at all possible.

* **Gross motor:** head control; sat alone; rolled over; pulled up; walked; climbed; kicked a ball; threw a ball; rode a tricycle; rode a bicycle; dressed and undressed self; toilet trained for bowel and bladder

* **Fine motor:** picking up a small object with the index finger and thumb; stacked blocks; tied shoes; printed letters; colored within lines; cursive writing

* **Language:** spoke single words; spoke sentences; started reading; articulated words

* **Other:** counted; knew the alphabet; knew colors; knew months of the year; knew birthday; knew telephone number; knew address

Medical History

Additionally, a medical history of this child during infancy, early childhood, and childhood should be given. There are a number of things that can happen to children during their early years that not only affect them but also affect their parents. Some of these are in the following list:

- **Hospitalizations:** whether for illnesses, accidents, or surgeries; length of stay; whether situation was life threatening

- **Emergency room:** whether for illnesses, accidents, poisonings, or other emergencies; any other emergency situations

- **Childhood illnesses:** any frequent illnesses such as chronic ear infections, gastrointestinal problems, respiratory problems, allergies, or asthma; any other infectious diseases or illnesses

- **Chronic illness:** what illness was or is; adjustment to the disease; whether there is good control of the disease; child adherence to the medical regimen; responsible party for child's care

- **Infectious diseases:** the diseases in question; how they were acquired (traveling?)

- **Immunizations:** immunizations received; unusual reactions such as high fevers, seizures, or significant irritability

- **High fevers:** cause of the fever; whether accompanied by seizures

- **Allergies:** what they're allergic to

- **Asthma:** whether asthma is present; level of control of condition

- **Medication:** what medication taken; child has own prescription or using someone else's; over-the-counter medications; reason for taking the medication

- **Headaches:** time of day of occurrences; location; usual duration; effective treatments; associated with vomiting; change in vision; staring spells; hearing changes

- **Stomachaches:** time of day of occurrences; vomiting; diarrhea; constipation; whether associated with blood or pus; factors that increase severity; factors that bring relief

* **Leg aches:** time of day of occurrences; presence of edema (swelling); stiffness; redness over the joints; fever associated with the pain; factors that bring relief

* **Chest pain:** time of day of occurrences; location of pain and whether pain radiates; effect of exercise on pain; associated with panic or anxiety; recent changes in activity level; dizziness or fainting

* **Fatigue:** amount of sleep; sleep locations; nightmares; interruptions at night; napping in school; medications that could be factors

Social and Family History

Your family and social history are of the utmost importance, but this is an area where many parents are hesitant to share. If you feel this way, perhaps it's because you don't understand the importance of the information or you're embarrassed by your information. Maybe you're afraid that your child is going to be like that relative of yours that ended up quitting school and getting in trouble with the law.

Initially, your therapist needs a clear picture of each member of the immediate family. It helps the therapist to understand how your child might relate to each individual family member. In order to understand this, the therapist should know the ages, health status, and educational status of all your children, and the relationship you have with them and specifically with the child you are concerned about. It is always good to know what your child likes to do with each parent, how they get along with their siblings, and what they worry about in relation to their mother, father, and siblings. I have found that when children begin telling me what they worry about regarding their parents and the child chooses to share that with their parents, their parents are usually very surprised that the child is even worried. Usually these worries surround such themes as finances, a parent's health problems, marital issues, or grieving issues. Through therapy, your child can learn to express these concerns with you rather than just keep them inside and worry about them. Not talking about these concerns can only lead to more stress and is likely to make the depression worse.

You may think you have protected your kids from worrying (or even knowing) about your family's finances, but you can be sure that they're very aware and thinking about financial matters in the home. Whatever the situation is, it may become a major contributor to the stress your child is feeling. Thus you should share at least the highlights of your financial situation with your psychologist or social worker. Try not to be insulted if they ask about it. In fact, it's so important that you should probably wonder if they *don't* ask you about it.

Immediate and extended family history also is very important since there is a genetic component to depression and many other mental-health problems. Any major history of physical illnesses such as neurological diseases (like brain tumors or seizures), endocrine disorders (like diabetes or hypo- or hyperthyroid) cancer, pulmonary disorders, cardiovascular disorders (for instance, heart disease or abnormal blood pressure) dermatological disorders (like eczema), gastrointestinal disorders (for example, abdominal pain, irritable bowel, or Crohn's disease), musculoskeletal disorders, and immunological disorders (like erythematous lupus) should be noted.

The family mental-health history should include an evaluation for attention deficit hyperactive disorder, alcoholism, substance abuse, depression, bipolar disorder, anxiety disorders, tic disorders, schizophrenia, mental hospitalizations, and suicide attempts or actual suicides. Of great importance is that you share if there is any known abuse (physical or sexual) to your child and, if you are willing, to share if anyone else in the family has suffered abuse.

Finally, it's important that your psychologist know if there have been any recent crises in this child's life. The death of a pet, a move, a house fire, a catastrophe either natural or man-made, a friend moving away, parent's divorce, the illness of a family member, or the death of a family member or friend. These, either alone or in combination with other life or personal circumstances, may result in a major behavioral upheaval.

Outside Reports

The team of professionals seeing and teaching your child should all be allowed and encouraged to communicate with each other. Make sure you let each professional know who is evaluating and treating your child. Although teachers and the school nurse are not part of the health team or the mental-health team, they are very important in the evaluation process. They may fill out diagnostic measures, provide a written observation record, share psycho-educational testing that has been done, perform requested psycho-educational testing, provide video tape of classroom behavior, carry out the classroom treatment intervention, and provide feedback on the treatment progress. In order for interaction and teamwork to take place for the best interest of your child, make sure you sign the necessary release of information forms.

Behavioral Assessments

There are some *self-report measures* (paper-and-pencil evaluations) that are generally collected by psychologists to determine how your child scores on scales that measure whether the likelihood of depression is present. There are other scales that show if there are signs and symptoms of other disorders in addition to the depression. These, along with the clinical evaluation, are used to determine the diagnosis. Your mental-health professional may prefer certain measures but the important thing is that you need to be quite honest when providing the information that is requested. Encourage your child to do the same.

The following are measures that are commonly used in the evaluation of children. These in no way are the only ones that are used in the clinical setting, but you should know about them in case you need to ask for their inclusion in your child's evaluation. Your mental-health professional will decide what is necessary for your child's evaluation.

Self-Report Measures

Self-report measures are those evaluations that are completed by you and your child. These include the following:

* *Schedule for Affective Disorders and Schizophrenia for School-Age Children—Present Episode (K-SADS-P):* This is an interview that is performed on the child and parent separately. The purpose is to determine if your child has depressive symptoms and the severity of those symptoms.

- *Child Behavior Checklist (CBCL):* This is a parent, youth, and teacher report to evaluate for depression, aggression, antisocial acts, and withdrawal behavior.

- *Children's Depression Inventory (CDI):* This measure looks at common symptoms seen in child and adolescent depression. Negative mood, interpretation problems, ineffectiveness, anhedonia, and negative self-esteem are measured. The *CDI* can be used to monitor changes in the child's depressive symptoms.

- *Behavior Assessment System for Children (BASC):* This is a self-report measure for the child, parents, and teacher that measures behavior and aspects of the personality. It also has a developmental history and a form for observing and recording classroom behavior. Such things as aggression, conduct problems, hyperactivity, attention problems, learning problems, anxiety, depression, somatization (physical complaints), atypicality, withdrawal, adaptability, leadership, social skills, and study skills are reported.

These are not the only measures. The *Eyberg Child Behavior Inventory, Conners Test, Piers-Harris Self-Concept Scale, Child Anxiety Scale,* and *Personality Inventory for Children—Revised* are also used in mental-health settings. These are used to rule out other disorders that the child may be suffering from along with the possible diagnosis of depression.

It's certainly not my purpose to tell your therapist what measures to use. My intention is to teach you that there are measures that can be used along with the clinical history. If medication or therapies are started without a careful evaluation then the treatment may be wrong because of an inaccurate diagnosis. Make sure no one other than a qualified mental-health professional evaluates you child very carefully.

Selecting Your Doctors and Therapists

You should never take it for granted that the doctor on your health insurance plan is necessarily the right one for your child. First of all, make sure that the doctors your child goes to have seen lots of children and that they recognize that depression occurs in children. Secondly, if they do not find a physical reason for your child's depression, then make sure they're open to the possibility that the problem could be emotional and are willing to refer you to or work with a therapist.

In general, you are constrained to a list your insurance company provides. Find out something about the professionals on the list. Sometimes the names are given but there is no indication if the individual sees children. You're going to need to find out. Ask your doctor, your child's teacher, school counselor, school social worker, or school psychologist, and any other professional that might have this knowledge about the reputations of possible therapists.

Other parents may sound like a good resource from your perspective. However, I caution you that if you ask these other parents, it will open up the potential for the "whole world" finding out your child's troubles, and it's really none of their business. Your child will not trust you if they find out you have "blabbed" to someone who might tell their son or daughter or other parents. So my advice is keep it between you and other professionals, or it could backfire on you. Then your child will have even bigger issues with his peers—and also with you. To put it bluntly, your child will have trouble trusting you and may even stop talking to you.

The Relationship with the Therapist

Once your child begins to see a therapist, then your job is twofold: to make sure that they are getting to their appointments and that getting good care. The evaluation is most important, so if the therapist begins to focus on the problem without a thorough history, you need to ask about it. The exception is if your child is actively suicidal and requires hospitalization. In that case a thorough history is still the foundation for helping your child, but is done after the child is made safe.

If you find yourself becoming suspicious about the questions being asked or irritated that the therapist is asking you personal questions about your social and family history, remember that this is a family affair. You cannot expect your child's therapist to treat your child in isolation from the other family members' problems and histories. If you still can't convince yourself that you as your child's parent need to be involved with the evaluation and therapy, then I would ask you to reconsider your position. Your child will not get better unless you and their other parent(s) are willing to become participants in the evaluation and treatment program. If you're not, you yourself may be a big reason that your child has a problem.

Once therapy is started then you can monitor how your child is doing. If you don't see improvement after a few weeks, it would be wise to ask the therapist how the overall therapy is going. A good therapist can answer this question and won't be insulted that you asked it. Keep in mind that it's perfectly okay to switch to another therapist if you're not satisfied with the first one. Make sure you have good reasons for doing this before you start your child all over, but trust your instincts when it appears that the therapist isn't the right person to treat your child.

Summary

In this chapter we have taken a look at the criteria for a diagnosis of depression in children. You've learned just how crucial you are in getting your child help, first with health professionals and second with the right mental-health professional. Your observations and the information you can provide about your child will make a significant contribution during the diagnostic process. An accurate diagnosis is the foundation for appropriate and successful treatment

The next chapter will help you understand the causes of depression. This information will help you assist your child in understanding what is going on with their feelings and that it will be something you can work together to control.

Chapter 3

What Causes Childhood Depression?

ഇ Jeff's Story

"I was afraid you were going to say that," the mother mumbled when I told her that Jeff's diagnosis was depression. "I have been a stay-at-home mother and he still is depressed." She began to cry. "We have given Jeff a good home. The only thing I can think of is that my sister tried to commit suicide when she was young. Maybe he got it from me. Is that possible?"

Parents may be devastated when their child is diagnosed with depression. After all, no one wants their child to be sad. You look for the reason, and most of the time you place a lot of blame on yourself. Well, you may have had something to do with it either through genetic inheritance or through circumstances in your child's life. Of course a child is going to inherit good and bad traits from their parents. Possibly they were exposed to a difficult life situation that they had trouble adjusting to. No matter what you think has caused this sadness, it would be very hard to point your finger at that one thing and say that it's the absolute reason for the depression. It may be a combination of factors, many of which you had no control over. What you do have control over is what you do about the depression. Obviously, you care or you wouldn't be taking action as you are right now. You are showing your child you do care and that is the most important message you can offer as they begin to recover from depression.

ഇ

What Is the Root of the Problem?

Doctors talk about the *etiology* of a medical diagnosis, which simply means the cause of the problem. Rarely is a disorder as complex as depression caused by just one thing; rather, it's the interaction of many factors in a person's life. You see people who never exercise avoid heart disease, while the guy who runs two marathons a year ends up in the hospital with a heart attack. Exercise may have played a role in overall heath, but it was that and its interaction with other factors in those individuals' lives that resulted in different endings. Your child is unique, has unique parents, lives in a unique environment, and has had unique life experiences. That is why they may have an emotional diagnosis whereas another child with similar circumstances looks to you like they are thriving. Their circumstances are similar but never exactly the same.

The Cause of Depression

What causes depression is not exactly known. It is thought that children's depression is caused by a combination of the same types of things that cause an adult's depression. These things include neurochemical factors, genetic factors, health factors, environmental factors, and cognitive factors. Each of these will be discussed more specifically.

Neurochemical Factors

Studies have indicated several neurotransmitter abnormalities in depression. First, let's take a look at how neurotransmitters work. The brain is made up of trillions of *neurons*, which are also referred to as "nerve cells." When a neuron is stimulated by a thought, it causes an electrical excitement. This electrical excitement goes from one neuron to another by traveling from the *dendrites*, which are like tree branches at the end of the neuron. A neuron usually has many dendrites. From the dendrites, the message travels over the cell body to the *axon* (which is a long, thin extension of the neuron) then on to the axon terminals, bulblike structures with sacs that contain the *neurotransmitters* (chemical

messengers). When the electrical impulse reaches the axon terminals, there is a release of the neurotransmitters that cross the *synapse* (space between the neurons), taking the electrical excitation
and message to the next neuron. The amount of the neurotransmitter is delicately balanced by either being reabsorbed by the
first neuron or broken down in the synapse and eventually
excreted from the body. If any part of this process becomes unbal-
anced then there may be a result of too much or too little of a
neurotransmitter. Because the neurotransmitter determines if a
message gets from neuron to neuron, not having enough means
that your nerve messages just aren't getting through (Tortora
2000). In the case when the neurotransmitter is serotonin and it is
low, the "feel good" messages don't get transmitted, and the person will end up with some or all of the symptoms of depression.

Genetic Factors

Studies show that depression tends to run in families. If you
have a family history of major depression, there is a significant
chance that your child will also develop depression. It's not only
more likely that depression will occur, but it is more likely to
come up at an earlier age and have a longer duration. Some very
interesting studies support the role of genetics in depression.

The research to support that heredity plays a key role in the
development of depression was done on adopted twins. The studies of adopted identical twins demonstrate that when they are
reared together, there is a concordance rate of 76 percent (both
individuals of the pair get depression) compared to 19 percent in
unidentical twins reared together. When identical twins were
reared apart, there was still a 67 percent concordance rate. This is
a strong argument for the significant role of genetics compared to
environmental influence in the development of depression. However, since both members were not *always* depressed, the study
also supports the argument that it is not just inheritance but also
other biological, social, and cognitive factors that play a part in
the cause of depression (Garfinkel et al. 1990). Clinicians and
researchers question whether some of these latter factors were the
result of the depression or whether the depression came as the
result of them. Research continues to attempt to answer this question. When the answer comes, it most likely will demonstrate that it
is probably both ways. Which comes first, the chicken or the egg?
They probably take turns.

Health Factors

Clearly, there are instances in a child's life when a new onset of a major illness or an accident resulting in long-term physical changes will trigger a diagnosis of *adjustment disorder*. Adjustment disorder is when a person develops behavioral or emotional symptoms in response to a specific stressor within three months of the beginning of that stressor. To qualify, these behavioral and emotional responses would be in excess of what would be expected as a response to that stressor and are seen as either an adjustment disorder with just depressive features (adjustment disorder with depressed mood) or an adjustment disorder with anxiety and depressive characteristics (adjustment disorder with mixed anxiety and depressed mood) (*DSM-IV-TR* 2000).

Additionally, the adjustment disorder needs to be carefully differentiated from the diagnosis of major depression. It might take some time for your professionals to do this, but it's important to separate the two so that your child can receive treatment that will relieve the symptoms while supporting the child in their adaptation to what has happened in their life. Your doctors and therapist will eventually make a diagnosis.

There are also events in a child's life such as the diagnosis of a life-threatening illness, experiences of abuse, or major accidents that result in post-traumatic stress disorder (PTSD), which to the uneducated eye may look like depression. (See chapter 7 for more about PTSD.) If you have a child who has experienced a devastating occurrence, you can ask the child's therapist to monitor your child for depression or one of the other associated diagnoses, such as PTSD. All too often this is not done because either you, as a parent, or your child perceive this as your doctor saying your child is "crazy" or will be "crazy." The fact is, the diagnostic process is a prevention step. It should be done as quickly as possible in relation to the traumatic event (new onset of disease, occurrence of an accident, and so forth) so that your child perceives it as support and not an indication that one more thing is going to be wrong with them.

In addition to the reaction to an illness, there are medical diagnoses that present with depressive symptoms according to Jellinek and Synder (1998). These include infections such as gram-negative sepsis (for example, an organism such as *E. coli* causing a blood infection), mononucleosis, influenza, encephalitis, pneumonia, hepatitis, and AIDS. Endocrine disorders, because of this system's close link to the central nervous system, are often associated with depressive symptoms or misdiagnosed as depression. They include new onset type 1 diabetes, poorly controlled diabetes, type 2 diabetes, adrenal gland dysfunction (like Addison's disease or Cushing's syndrome), thyroid dysfunction (for example, hypothyroidism), abnormal testosterone, and a change in estrogen and progesterone levels. Precocious puberty during early childhood or the onset of puberty during late childhood are likely to present with irritability, tearfulness, and mood swings, along with the physical changes. Electrolyte imbalances such as low sodium and low potassium may result in mood changes. Neurological disorders that include brain tumors, seizures, postictal period (the time following a seizure), post head injury, post encephalitis, post-cerebrovascular accidents, multiple sclerosis (rare in children), and Huntington's disease may look like depression. Other diseases that may mimic depression include autoimmune diseases (fatigue is common), certain malignancies (the depressive symptoms may be an early sign), anemia, leukemia, Wilson's disease (a very rare disease in which there is excessive copper storage leading to liver diseases), porphyria, and uremia. Additionally, alcohol and drug use may result in symptoms that look like depression. Other times, alcohol or drugs may be used as a self-medication for depression (Jellinek and Snyder 1998).

There are a number of medications, both prescribed and over-the-counter, that can also cause depressive symptoms. If you look in the *Physician's Desk Reference (PDR)* for 2002, you would probably notice that depression is listed as a side effect for many drugs. Even if the medication your child is taking has only a very low occurrence of depressive symptoms as a side effect, don't rule it out as a possible cause. It still has the potential of being the culprit in mimicking depression. Always watch and listen to your child closely whenever they start taking a medicine. Drugs may have side effects you and your doctor were not counting on. Children whose parents or siblings have unusual reactions to the same classification of drugs or drugs in general have an even greater chance of being at risk for side effects.

Some specific medications that commonly cause depressive symptoms are steroids, antihypertensives, barbiturates, birth-control pills, testosterone, gastrointestinal medications, benzodiazepines, antiseizure medications, cimetidine, aminophylline, clonidine, digitalis, and thiazide diuretics (Jellinek and Snyder 1998). Even those drugs that have been cited in the literature as causing depression have no studies to support these claims with children. In spite of this, these drugs should still be considered as potential stimulants of depression in children.

Many times substance abuse and alcohol use will start after the first bout of depression. Patients will tell their doctor that the abuse was their attempt to find a way to self-medicate, as an attempt to cope with life situations. The underlying depression may not be noticed until your child is withdrawing from the alcohol or drug, at which time the disorder will rear its head again.

You may be wondering whether drugs and alcohol are really an issue for children. I want to emphasize that it is more and more common for school-age children to use drugs and alcohol than in the past. Children who live in families where there is very little support and attend schools where the same is true may resort to other individuals and ways to get support. Substance abuse may be one of those ways.

Environmental Factors

It is extremely difficult to separate the environmental factors from the genetic factors when establishing the basis of a child's depression, but it's clear that stressful situations can culminate and result in an individual being depressed. Depressed kids often feel helpless and unable to reach out for help. In some situations, they feel unable to get out of their specific living conditions. Researchers have compared the lack of motivation to cope in certain situations as being similar to some qualities of depression.

Let's take a closer look at some of the more common stressors facing children that often result in depression or an adjustment disorder with depressive symptoms. This is not an exhaustive list but I think it will help you get an idea of what to look out for.

Family matters. Parents having a difficult time in their marriage is a common concern of children. You may think you're effectively hiding marital problems from your child, but I wouldn't count on it. Children can always pick up when there are problems between their mom and dad. After all, they have lived with you for years and know your behaviors. Even if you think you are discussing your problems behind closed doors, it's very likely your child has overheard, whether intentionally or not, your discussions. Even if they haven't heard or understood the words, they've undoubtably noticed the emotion in your voices during a discussion or argument. From there, it's easy to jump to the conclusion that you're getting divorced. After all, half of their friends' parents are divorced, so why not you? With this idea firmly in mind, your child may begin to avoid school, act out at school and at home, and shows signs of lower self-esteem or even depression. They make every attempt through their behavior to control things. But instead of gaining control from these acting-out behaviors, they begin to feel more out of control and helpless.

It has always amazed me how many children know when their mother or father is having an affair. Many times this is before the other spouse knows. You may wonder how they detect this. Well, your child is probably good at picking up hints about their environment and, quite frankly, you may not be very good at hiding what you're doing. You and your spouse might be in denial, but your child is not. They may not know whom it is with but they "sense" it is with someone. Then it makes perfectly good sense to the child that if they cause trouble maybe their parent will have to stay home to control the situation. They believe that through misbehavior, or even a suicide attempt, they can keep their parents together.

You may be one of the parents that has already taken the big step and gotten divorced. Though it may be painful to acknowledge, I can guarantee you, your child will probably feel that in some way they are responsible for the failed marriage. In their eyes, they've been abandoned. That child will go through a grief response that is similar to one that they would experience if they were to lose you through death. If you died, your child would get some extra attention, but many times a divorce results in less attention because after all, the parents are not dead—they just live in two different home environments. Your child may become the conduit for the messages between you and your former spouse and might at times even be a spy. At times they are caught between your arguments over visitation and child support and thus may end up being a peacemaker. In the event one parent gets married, then the child has lost all hope for getting their parents back together. You can see the hopelessness and helplessness your child may come to feel and how this might set them up for subsequent behavioral and emotional problems. Your child has no time to worry about their academics, sports, and friends when they are worried about their parents childish conflicts. They may all too often be pushed into being a parent's confidant. And we wonder why these children are stressed.

It may not be the parents who are having the problems but a sibling, usually an older sibling. They may be sneaking out at night, not going to school, using drugs, having sex, plus a number of other things. I've seen many cases where the younger child stays up at night worrying about their sibling because they know about these behaviors when you don't. Many times, your child holds these secrets about their siblings close to their heart because they're afraid of what would happen if you or your spouse find out. The child often starts feeling responsible for the sibling. They also begin to feel responsible for the discipline of the sibling because, in their eyes, you aren't interested.

The alcoholic parent or the addicted parent leaves their children without the ability to predict how the parent is going to react to certain situations such as school grades, athletic performance, home chores, and day-to-day behavior. Children in these situations go around walking on eggshells. These kids begin to perceive the world in the same way, thinking "If my parent is unpredictable, then everyone else in the world is unpredictable."

You also might be struggling with your own mood disorder, either depression or bipolar disorder, either treated or untreated. Children whose parents refuse to admit that they have a problem are less likely to be taken for help. In the event that you do try to get help for your child, it may not be successful until you or your spouse get therapy for yourselves. Not only has your behavior taught your child that therapy is not necessary but also your problems undermine the treatment attempts of your therapist. The question becomes whether the child really is depressed or if they're reacting to the parents' mood disorder. Would your child recover if you as their parent got help?

Children in a family where there is illness also are at high risk for depression. If a parent or sibling has a major illness, the child worries about what will happen. Many times I've seen parents or a sibling with poorly controlled diabetes. Your child may witness hypoglycemic attacks that they feel responsible to treat. They worry that if they're not able to treat it right that this loved one may end up dying—and it will be all the child's fault. Your child may have a parent with cancer or an autoimmune disease.

They not only worry about the ill parent and what will happen to them but also wonder what will happen if that parent dies. Will the other parent be next? Then the child starts feeling very guilty about wondering if a parent is going to die and worries that these feelings and thoughts may in fact contribute to the death of a parent in some way. Pretty heavy thoughts for anyone, much less for a child, to have.

Along the same lines is the child who actually has an immediate member of their family die. Surviving children feel a significant amount of guilt and wonder if in some way they are being punished by God for something they have done, said, or thought. Depression is a natural part of the bereavement process and may or may not be resolved. Some children have to be seen by a therapist while others do well with a support group or their family and friends. What is known is that if children lose a parent or a sibling, the likelihood for depression later in their lives is very high. Realistically, if you have lost your spouse or a child, you probably don't have a lot of energy to give to the surviving children. They may feel abandoned or left alone and feel an additional responsibility to make it all right for you. Children often try to take the dead parent's place or try to fill in for the dead sibling. In any case, this is a very difficult job, one that must be overwhelming for any child. It's a job that may set up the child for depression.

If none of these things are happening in your family but you still have a depressed child then you need to ask yourself if any type of abuse is going on, such as physical, mental, or sexual abuse. I am always astonished at how insulted parents are when I ask this question. The fact is, in 1995 there were three million reports of possible abuse. One million of those were substantiated. This is believed to be underreported (Ludwig and Rostain 1999).

I am also saddened at how some parents deny the possibility that this could have been done to their child. I've seen some parents who may, in the past, have questioned whether their child has been or is being sexually abused, but because their child has not shared it with them, they deny that it is even a possibility. It's important to realize that many times a child feels that they can't tell their parent because that child has been threatened and believes that if they tell the truth then something terrible will happen to members of their family. Perpetrators also commonly blame the children for the abuse happening. What is a child to do? They usually respond by acting out or becoming quite depressed. This behavior is a scream for help.

Family financial concerns also are something kids commonly worry about. They don't understand the situation and dwell on why they can't have some of the things they want. In other situations, they worry about a parent's job loss or the possibility of such a loss. They hear their parents whisper about not having enough money to pay the bills or the chance of losing their home. Kids in this position wonder, "How can I live without a home. Where will I sleep? Where will I play? Will my friends make fun of me?"

School situations. Children spend the majority of their time at school, learning and playing. They learn academic subjects, how to get along with people, and how to play certain playground games, including the art of negotiation. There is, however, always a child or two that is not included, and who is the target of teasing by the class or by the class bully. This can happen at any age during the school years. It might be hard for your child to go to school if they don't feel liked by the other kids in their class. It is even harder if they feel singled out by bullies. They may be scared and may even have been threatened with violence if they tell the teacher. Unfortunately, bullies are very good at restricting their teasing and threatening to times when the teacher is not around. You might hear from the teacher, "Your child is not paying attention. They don't seem to be getting work done." But from a child's perspective, it's a little hard to concentrate on academic subjects when the most important thing is to survive and to be included in the playground games, to sit by the "popular" kids at lunch, and to be included on the birthday invitation list for the upcoming weekend. The social aspect of school becomes more important than the subjects. After all, none of us wants to be lonely.

Learning can be difficult for certain children. Your child may suffer from an actual learning disability in one or several subject areas or because of attention deficit hyperactivity disorder they may not be able to focus long enough to learn (see chapter 7). Like I said earlier, the child might also be preoccupied with not being included in the social group of the class and can't pay attention. You also have to consider if your child is bored with their school subjects and needs to be challenged with more advanced subjects. It's hard to go to school if school is either hard or boring. If the adults in their life tend to scold them for not performing to the best of their ability, your child may begin to experience burn-out and believe that no one cares about them. Such children suffer from teachers and parents not assessing why they don't perform better. All too often they are judged to be lazy, even though it's really very unusual for a child to be lazy. Something else is going on, and it behooves you and the teacher to figure it out.

Cognitive factors

I have given you multiple examples of factors that may result in depression or, at the very least, depressive symptoms. Throughout these examples I have also talked about how the child perceives and thinks about those situations to which they are exposed. The child's thoughts are directly related to their feelings, and some of these thoughts are automatic and without a lot of evidence. As far as the child thinks, what they perceive is fact. These perceptions may be distorted and, if they're skewed in a negative way, may lead to the likelihood of depressed feelings. Other times the child generalizes from one situation to all similar situations and in some cases dissimilar situations ("If Tommy's parents are splitting up, then maybe mine will, too"). They can't help but have negative thoughts about these situations, thus again leading to some negative feelings. Helping a child with their thoughts so that they can be more accurate can result in more positive feelings. This will be discussed in more detail in chapter 6.

Summary

Depressive symptoms and actual depression can result from a number of factors. These range from heredity to illnesses to side effects from medications and illicit drugs. Various family or school problems are also key reasons for consideration when a child suffers from behavior problems, depressive symptoms, or actual depression. What is evident is the interaction of all of these factors and the role of how the child perceives them. These factors play an important role in the development of depression.

The next chapter is an overview of the different types of treatments for a child with depression. This will be the foundation for subsequent chapters that will be more specific regarding your role in helping your depressed child.

Chapter 4

First Things First: What To Do for Your Child

∞ *Gina's Story*

"I am so mad at my doctor. He insists that Gina is depressed and he can fix it if I fill a prescription for an antidepressant. Don't you think that's a little premature? She can't be that depressed."

Gina's parents knew that Gina had been having major problems in school. She was always getting suspended from school for fighting with her classmates. The teachers couldn't believe how angry this ten-year-old girl seemed to be. They knew she had been a foster child and had been recently adopted by her foster parents. Little did they know how much this ten-year-old girl had packed into her short life. She was one of three children who lost their mother in an automobile accident. Their father reared them until he became ill and required nursing-home care. They had no other family, and so they were placed in foster homes. Now, after three years of foster care, a wonderful couple had adopted them. The only concern that the couple had was Gina's disposition. She was a smart little girl. Until this year she had always made Cs and Bs, but now she seemed to be struggling with all of her subjects. She was lucky if she made a C. Her adoptive parents related this to her refusal to do her schoolwork. No matter what they did to encourage her, she wouldn't do her schoolwork. She would much rather come home and take a nap. She would wake up only long enough to pick at her food and then go back to bed. She was rarely called by a classmate and was never included in any of the birthday parties or sleepovers.

Gina's parents reasoned that anyone would be sad if their classmates didn't include them but that it wouldn't necessarily make them depressed. They felt Gina's doctor was making a really big assumption. It *seemed to them that prescribing an antidepressant was a big step to take, especially when they felt Gina hadn't been adequately evaluated. Weren't there blood tests that could be done to make this diagnosis?*

These are not uncommon responses for doctors or parents in this situation. Maybe your doctor, or you for that matter, doesn't know the different things that can be done for a child with depressive symptoms. You may need to try some things besides medicine at first and then add the medicine to those treatments. If you only give your child antidepressants, it may add to the child's feelings of hopelessness. It can also give your child a message that drugs are the answer to all of your problems, and that they don't have to do anything for themselves. Our culture already tells our children that, so why do the same thing with your vulnerable child?

℘

Diagnosing the Problem

Chapter 2 reviewed what measures need to be completed before making a diagnosis of depression. Obviously, the clinical diagnosis is very important and may not need the support of additional measures, especially if your child is talking about wanting to die. The message I want to get across to you is that your child needs to have an evaluation by their medical doctor first. If the doctor feels your child is depressed, then you and your child need to see a mental-health professional. Their training can help your child identify what is troubling them so that adequate interventions can be initiated. Now let's look at some of your options.

Medications and Hospitalization

Medications will be discussed in detail in chapter 8, but an initial step is to decide whether they are indicated at all. This discussion should take place with your doctor since you are both part of the team taking care of your child. If your child is crying all the time, not sleeping at all, having major acting-out problems, and is talking about being better off dead or wanting to die, then you most likely need to follow your doctor's advice about medication. At the same time, go ahead and ask the doctor for the name of a therapist who can see you and your child. It's very important to add therapy to the course of medication because no pill is going to be the only thing to cure your child, especially if they are suicidal. Something more needs to be done. In some of these more serious situations, you might have to consider placing your child on an in-patient psychiatric ward in order to keep them safe and so they can receive intensive therapy for the depression. I know you may feel that hospitalizing your child would be the worst thing you can imagine. You may even wonder how you could deal with sharing this with your family and friends. But the pain and possible embarrassment over sharing this information really can't be your first concern. You need to worry about keeping your child safe and alive. A death is not what you want to share.

If your child is not actively suicidal and does not require hospitalization, it's still important that your doctor, school psychologist, or school social worker draw up a suicide-prevention contract with your child. This contract should clearly state that your child would contact a responsible person such as yourself or call 911 if they begin thinking about suicide. The contract should look something like this.

Suicide-Prevention Contract

Date _____

I _____ ,

promise to tell my parent, _____ ,

or my school counselor, _____ ,

if I think about killing myself. The numbers where I can reach

them are _____ ,

and _____ .

If I cannot reach them, then I will call the police at 911.

Child's signature _____

Parent's signature _____

Witness signature _____

Although the research has not been done to demonstrate if this clearly stops a child from killing themselves, it is my experience and many other mental-health professionals' experience that it does make the child stop and think before they impulsively attempt suicide. It gives the child a safety net to fall back on if they start becoming hopeless and think that death is their only alternative, helping them realize that they are not alone and that there are people there to help them when they need it.

Finding Your Child's Therapist

If your child is safe enough to stay at home and attend school, then the next important thing for you to do is find a good therapist who you both can relate to. Your doctor or school counselor may have some ideas about who to see. Networking with parents who have had similar situations is also helpful if you're secure that your business won't end up being the town topic of gossip. You may be restricted to the list of providers that your insurance company offers. In this case, you can give that list to your doctor or another professional, such as the school nurse or counselor, who might know other people who have been to some of these therapists.

I believe it's important that you and your child both like your child's therapist. There are people who would argue that the only person who has to like the therapist is the child. But suppose you don't like the therapist. This situation will make it much easier to mistrust the therapist and may even start to undermine the work this therapist and your child are trying to do. For instance, it may become far too easy for you to miss taking your child to their appointments.

Another reason it's important to find a therapist you respect is because, in a large way, they are your therapist, too. Your child's therapist will be helping you learn how to help your child. There may be times when both parents will be involved in sessions on learning to discipline your child or helping to improve your child's self-esteem. There are other times that family therapy will be required. None of these different types of therapy needed by your child or needed by you and your child can be successful if you cannot relate to the therapist. This is about the entire family helping the child during a time of illness and crisis, so make sure you all can relate to the therapist.

Behavior Therapy

Behavior interventions can be used when you need an effective way to discipline your child. Remember, children with depressive symptoms may be very irritable and resistant to change. Discipline based on behavioral principles makes the assumption that all behavior is learned behavior and that the unacceptable behavior can be changed. These techniques aren't just punishing your child but are teaching your child what to do and what not to do. *Operant conditioning* (in which behaviors are controlled by consequences) and classical conditioning are key components of behavior therapy. This form of consistent discipline will give your child support and the ability to know what is expected of them. Children who feel this support will generally develop stronger self-esteem. The basics of discipline based on behavioral principles will be discussed in chapter 5.

Cognitive Therapy

Cognitive therapy, initially developed for adults, emphasizes helping the individual to identify and change negative and maladaptive beliefs. According to Beck et al. (1979) and other early cognitive researchers, depressed people look at the world in a distorted way. These distortions or irrational thoughts are deeply embedded in the way the person thinks and are connected to the way the person feels. This way of thinking is used by everyone at some time and often becomes a bad habit. However, the depressed person thinks in this way more than most of us. Cognitive therapy aims at helping the person identify and change their distorted way of looking at something. Because the way we think directly affects the way we feel, changing negative thoughts can result in a lighter mood. It is believed that children as young as eight years can begin to learn these cognitive techniques. More specifics will be discussed in chapter 6 so that you might use some cognitive techniques to help your child.

Family Therapy

Family therapy may be necessary for those families that have more complex problems. For example, these problems might include a parent with depression, a parent or sibling with alcoholism, or parents experiencing marital difficulties. Parents or siblings diagnosed with a major physical illness may also benefit from family therapy. Family therapy aims at opening communication up between the family members. It also helps individuals recognize their own problems and how these affect other family members. Many different approaches are taken for family therapy. It may be necessary that the child and a parent have individual therapy at the same time as the family is involved in their therapy. You should ask your therapist whether they feel qualified and experienced to do both, or if your child and family should have two different therapists.

If problems can't be successfully treated with therapy in an office setting, then home therapy may need to be considered. Some therapy offices provide these services. There are also agencies that will place a family therapist in your home to not only do family therapy but also help solve some of the more difficult problems that may surround your child's acting-out behavior. This is not Big Brother watching you. It is, rather, a professional who hopes to prevent more serious problems from occurring by coaching the parents in discipline techniques at the time of the misbehavior. It might prevent you from abusing your child when you are at your wits end with your child's behavior and irritability.

Support Groups

Support groups may help you or a family member when there are problems that coexist with you child's depression. For instance, you might find that a support group for chronic illnesses can be very helpful if your family is living with chronic illness. Frequently, there are separate groups for the caregivers and for the children in these families. Whether it's chronic illness, substance abuse, or some other problem that affects the family, try not to look at these groups as just one more thing you have to do. They are quite educational and they allow family members to develop a network of support with people who are experiencing similar challenges in their lives.

If your family has a member who suffers from drug addiction or alcoholism, you might want to find a treatment center and a support group for your loved one. It's likely that each family member will also benefit from these same types of support. Your therapist, school counselor, or school nurse should be excellent resources for identifying appropriate support groups. An example of a type of support group for these types of problems would be Alcoholics Anonymous. The individual with alcoholism gets help, but there is also Alanons (for the spouse) and Alateens (for the children), both support groups.

Bereavement support groups may also be helpful for your family if you have experienced the loss of a loved one. Compassionate Friends is an example of this type of group and may be helpful for you or members of your family. Many times this group is a good resource to find other, more specialized bereavement groups or for groups for your child or children.

Parent's Individual Therapy

Do you suffer from a psychiatric diagnosis or think you do? Do you feel stressed to the hilt because of your children, marital problems, or job problems? Then you would benefit from your own individual counseling. You might be amazed at how much better your family will do if you get help for yourself. At times, you may even benefit from medication. This might help with your mood or your anxiety about the problems in your family. Remember, you are a role model for your children. If you don't seek help, your child is unlikely to be willing to get help either.

Here are some of the signs to watch for that may indicate that you could benefit from individual therapy:

- You find yourself with negative thoughts and negative feelings.

- You had a mood disorder when you were young.

- You have made a suicide attempt earlier in your life.

- You have a history of postpartum depression.

- There are marital difficulties.

- A member of your family suffers from a chronic or life-limiting illness.

- A member of your family suffers from mental illness.

- Your child requires numerous trips to your primary-care physician.

- You find yourself going to your doctor frequently for multiple physical complaints, which may be a sign of stress or your own depression.

- You find yourself napping and sleeping increased hours at night.

- You have sleep disturbances.

- Your appetite has changed (increased or decreased).

- You are not getting your responsibilities done (home or professional).

- You experience panic attacks.

- You have dropped social relationships or are socially isolated.

- You don't feel support from an outside source.

- You feel hopeless.

- You feel guilty regarding most things.

- You feel worthless.

- You have thoughts of dying or committing suicide.

- You've recently lost your job.

- You're experiencing major financial problems.

Now that we've looked at a brief introduction to the different type of mental-health interventions for you and your child, let's look at some school considerations that need to be a part of the plans to help your child.

School Considerations

Often school holds the answer to why your child is feeling so depressed. Children who don't feel a part of the action at school have a hard time getting up in the morning and attending classes in what they perceive as an unfriendly environment (see chapter 7 for a description of anxiety that may lead to school avoidance). For instance, children many times are the targets of teasing. These may be children with special needs, or they may simply be the new kid on the block. At times certain children are the target of just one or two bullies, and other times a child feels that the whole class is making fun of them. This may just be a distorted thought, or it could be a very rational belief if your child has trouble in school or suffers from some type of physical problem. Generally speaking, teachers intervene when a child is being teased, but sometimes they may need a reminder that protection is part of their job. It can be hard for teachers to always know what's going on in their class if they aren't on playground duty at the time the bullying is going on. You may also find that the teacher has the philosophy that the children need to work out their own problems. I believe teachers need to be involved and then decide how the child needs to work out his conflicts with his peers. As a parent, you need to demand such involvement. Keep in mind that teasing does more harm to developing self-esteem than violence (Feinberg 1996), especially if your child doesn't feel supported by their peers or teachers. And if bullies are allowed to keep up their bullying, they may actually be learning some very unhealthy ways of relating to their peers. Kids who are allowed to bully are five times more likely than their peers to have major behavior problems as they get older. Additionally, as adults they are more likely to have children who have aggression problems (Feinberg 1996).

Lessons Learned from Teasing

If a teased child has support from the adults in their environment, then teasing can be used to teach the child some important lessons about life. Feinberg (1996) suggests that the following lessons might be learned from teasing:

* Negotiating

* Using humor

* Ignoring and leaving a confrontation

* Problem solving

* Getting help from authority

* Using the cognitive strategy of self-talk (see chapter 6)

* Sticking up for themselves

* Informing authorities if they are being teased or another child is being teased

* Letting bullies know that they are going to be told on

Also, remember how important it is for you to help your child have friends over so that you can help them learn social skills. If your child is new at school, you might ask the teacher for a suggestion for a new friend to have over. Sometimes a bully teases your child because they don't have the foggiest idea how to make friends. If the teacher thinks this is the case, then you might want to consider actually having the bully to your home. Then you can see firsthand what is going on and you might discover that wanting your child as a friend is all the bully was after in the first place.

Academic Supports

Let's say your child not only has depression but also suffers from a disability as a result of the depression or suffers from another disability, such as a learning disability. What are your child's rights?

The Individuals with Disabilities Education Act (IDEA)

You might wonder what your child's educational rights are. Let's say you are wondering if your child has a learning disability. You can ask your school to evaluate your child. This request should be done in writing, because you should have a record of your requests. This request should go to your child's principal or to the school district's director of special education. You will be requesting that a comprehensive evaluation be completed with your child. The school does not *have* to do the testing but in the event the school refuses then they must let you know in writing why they have declined. If you want to appeal this decision, the school must provide you a written explanation of how the appeal system works and how to submit an appeal. Additionally, each state has a Parent Training and Information (PTI) center. This resource will help you determine your rights under the law and how they relate to your request. On the other hand if the public agency (school) wants to initiate testing for your child, they must notify you in writing. You, then, must give permission for the testing to be conducted (National Information Center for Children and Youth with Disabilities 1999a).

Let's assume that the school agrees that there is a need for the evaluation to be done. What can you expect?

* A written notification of your child's rights and your rights and how to appeal if you have a grievance. This is called *Procedural Safeguards* or *Due Process Rights*.

* An evaluation aimed at determining your child's strengths and educational needs.

* If your child qualifies, a written plan for instruction for your child.

* An evaluation provided free of charge.

* That the evaluation will be conducted in your child's native language, including sign language.

* Your written permission is required to conduct the evaluation.

* You will have input into the evaluation.

* An evaluation group which consists of you, your child's classroom teacher, a special-education teacher, a school administrator; someone who can interpret the test and the implications of the results, your child, other professionals if necessary (like the school psychologist, the occupational therapist, a physical therapist, or a speech or hearing specialist), members of your medical team, and your mental-health professional.

The evaluation will be conducted with observation, testing, interviews of the child, and information gathered from parents, outside professionals, and past school records.

The Individual with Disabilities Education Act (IDEA), a federal law, states that schools are responsible for providing specific steps they'll take to meet your child's needs if they are determined to meet one of thirteen disability categories. According to the National Information Center for Children and Youth with Disabilities (1999b), the categories of disabilities according to the IDEA are

* Autism
* Deafness
* Deaf-blindness
* Hearing impairment

- Mental retardation

- Multiple disabilities

- Orthopedic impairment

- Other health impairment (OHI)

- Serious emotional disturbance

- Specific learning disability

- Speech or language impairment

- Traumatic brain injury

- Visual impairment, including blindness

If, after the comprehensive evaluation by the school, your child is found eligible for special education, your school team and you will write an Individualized Education Program (IEP) for your child. An IEP is an educational plan that tells you how, when and where your child will be taught, and who will be meeting the unique needs of your child. The IEP's purpose is setting learning goals for your child and stating how the school will provide services for your child. This must be done within thirty days after your child is found eligible.

Once the IEP has been established by the evaluation team, then a meeting will be called within thirty days to review the written stated goals. Your child must be reevaluated every three years according to the IDEA. The IDEA also requires an annual meeting to review your child's progress on their IEP and to determine if there are any changes that have to be made. And bear in mind that you don't have to wait until the teachers call the annual meeting. You, the teacher, or any other school professional may call a meeting at any time.

Section 504 of the Rehabilitation Act of 1973

Section 504 is a civil rights act and part of the Rehabilitation Act of 1973. Like the IDEA, it will protect your child if they have a disability. The section allows your child to receive the free public education that would be conducted with students without disabilities. It ensures that your child is not discriminated against. It also requires your school district to make accommodations to allow your child the right and ability to have an "equal opportunity to participate in school and school-related activities" (Kansas

State Department of Education 2001). Disability is defined as "any physical or mental impairment that results in your child being limited in one or more of life's major activities" (Kansas State Department of Education 2001). Each school district is required to designate a Section 504 coordinator. What can be considered a disability may be a chronic disease, congenital defects, mental-health problems, head injury, and so forth. If the school determines either by their own observations or through information from the parents that a student has a disability, then an evaluation for eligibility under Section 504 should be conducted. Unlike the IDEA evaluation requirements, the Section 504 evaluation is not a test but rather a gathering of information.

If your child is found to be eligible under Section 504, then special accommodations and programs are designed to meet your child's unique needs in the regular classroom. Some examples of these accommodations are

* An extra set of books

* Adaptation of assignments

* Special seating

* Availability of a modified school bus

* Peer tutors

* Modified physical education

* Assistance in administration of medication

These are just a few of the accommodations that can be made. You and your child can be a part of the Section 504 meetings. In the event your child is not found to be eligible for these benefits and you disagree, you have a right of appeal. According to the Kansas State Department of Education (2001), you may appeal in the following way:

* First talk to your teacher about any differences you have with the school

* Request mediation for these differences

* Set up a meeting with your school district's Section 504 coordinator

* Set up a meeting with your school superintendent

* Contact your local parent advocacy group

- Request a hearing, if necessary
- File a complaint with your Office for Civil Rights

So now you know that your child has a right to an equal opportunity for the same education as any other child. It's important to know your rights. If you would like more detailed literature, contact the National information Center for Children and Youth with Disabilities (contact information is in the Resources section). If your child qualifies for special services or support, it may make a difference in how your child views school and how the school views your child.

Summary

We've been investigating the varieties of therapeutic interventions for your child and you. One of the main points I'd like you to take away from this chapter is that a pharmacological intervention should not be used alone but rather with individual or family therapy. I also advocate the use of support groups for your family so a network of understanding and supportive people is available to you. Support to families while they are in crisis or under a significant amount of stress has been shown to result in more positive outcomes.

Usually your child will take their cues from you when deciding whether they'll go along with getting therapeutic help. If you or the child's other parent have significant mental or physical health problems and have not done much about them, then it is likely that your child will respond in the same manner. Always remember that your actions speak louder than your words.

We've also looked at the special school programs that offer necessary services for your child if needed. This information will make you a better advocate for your child while considering their unique needs. Without the knowledge of these programs, your child could be attending school without everything they require.

As you've most likely realized, your child's problem is a family problem requiring changes in the way your whole family is living. In response to these needs, the next chapter will look at changes parents need to make in their approach to parenting. We'll be taking an especially close look at very effective behavioral interventions for discipline. In my experience, these techniques are practical ways so you can jump in and help your child.

Chapter 5

Discipline and Your Child

➣ *David's Story*

"I am so tired of having to tell David five or six times to do something and even then he does not do exactly what I want him to do. He gets mad when I tell him it's not done the way I wanted it done, so I do it—it's just easier to do it myself."

David is nine years old and the only child of divorced parents. He has learned that he can get lots of gifts from his father, Mike, when he stays with him on weekends. Much of the time spent with his father during his visitation is going to movies, going out to dinner, and buying toys that David feels he simply must have. David seems very angry and irritable to Mike. When Mike asks him to do a chore, David gets mad and yells, "This is the weekend! I don't want to do it." So Mike feels that it is easier to do it himself and let David just rest. Mike thinks David is bored there and that this feeling will inevitably lead to trouble. He hates having to discipline David during their time together since David is only with him every other weekend. After all, why not make it a positive weekend rather than one in which there are tears, yelling, and pouting? Neither one of them has fun when there's conflict. Mike does tell him that if he doesn't behave, they won't be going to the movie, but there are few chores or opportunities for David to get into trouble at his dad's. However, when David does do something wrong, he knows that they'll still go to the movies. Mike never follows through with his warnings.

When David is at home with his mother, things aren't much different. He has chores, homework assignments, curfews, and a number of rules to follow. His Mom feels like she is always walking on eggshells with him to get him to do these things. David frequently reminds his mother that he never has to do anything for his dad and he likes being

there better than at home because, "Dad never yells at me like you do."
Also he is frequently heard saying that he would rather live at his dad's.
His mother doesn't know how to respond to him. She wishes she could
provide recreational activities, but most of her time is spent trying to get
him to do his homework and clean up his room. It always ends up in a
screaming match. Frankly, it's not much fun to even come home from
work and face David. He's irritable and won't behave. If he's not sleep-
ing, then he is on his computer. He always want to be by himself. His
mother feels like she's a terrible parent, nagging her son all of the time.
She wishes he would just do what she asked him to the first time.

This is a very common scenario that I hear in my office several
times a week. It demonstrates how frustrating some children can be and
who is really in command at home. Frequently, it's the child. Clearly,
this boy gets what he wants by getting mad. He gets his mother to do his
chores and to quit nagging him. She even feels guilty that she is always
asking him to do something. All of this drama means there is very little
downtime to just enjoy each other. She hates seeing him and he hates
seeing her. In David's eyes, his mother is always making him do some-
thing. She isn't fun like she used to be. She never wants to do anything
fun like his dad does. She just wants to work all the time around the
house. She is always a nag.

ℰↃ

Parents As Disciplinarians

As you can see, David's behavior exemplifies a lot of sadness. He
is trying desperately to control the situation through his behavior.
He is noncompliant, irritable, and feels his mother is always nagging him and making him do something. Often parents in these
situations feel sorry for their child because of the divorce. The
parents' guilt takes over their common sense. Discipline is either
neglected, or if done, it is on an inconsistent basis. Children in
these situations actually begin to feel frightened. When the parent
begins to feel they are losing control, the child senses this. How
frightening is it for the child to not receive consistent discipline?
Think what you would feel like if suddenly there were no laws
for you to abide by, no guidance about how to behave. Most
likely, it would make you feel pretty insecure. Well, that is how
your child probably feels if suddenly the discipline is lacking or

inconsistent (for instance, after their parents get divorced). It's just one more thing for them to deal with.

So how do you get through these times? The answer is clear but not necessarily simple. It would be nice if you became a good, consistent disciplinarian. Discipline is two-sided. One side is the positive feedback you give your child for their appropriate behavior. A sad child needs all the positives they can get. The other side is the punishment part of the discipline. This allows you to help your child control their behavior and reassure them that you are in control, not them. So let's start now.

When parents say they need a manual to raise their children they're really not far from the truth. Certain principles can be identified for rearing children, but in all instances you as a parent need to know your child. You are the one who knows when they're acting out and when they act like something is bothering them. They become irritable, angry, and belligerent when you ask them to do something. Even if something else is bothering them or you know they're depressed, lonely, and struggling in school, you still need to send the message that you care enough to discipline them.

Imagine that you have a terrible cold and are driving to work feeling as though you're in a daze. You run a red light and a police officer sees you do it. They pull you over and you say, "I'm sorry officer, but I am sick." Do you think the police officer is going to say, "I'm so sorry you're feeling bad. I'll let you off this time"? You can be about 99 percent sure that's not going to happen. The officer will still give you a ticket for running the light. You're pretty sure that if you run a red light in front of a police officer that they will ticket you. They are consistent and really don't feel sorry for you. Well guess what? Your child needs to anticipate that same consistent discipline. Then they will think twice before they say no to your request because they can count on you to give them discipline.

Defining Discipline

Discipline is usually equated with corporal punishment. You may be saying right now, "But I don't want to spank my child. They're too big to discipline." This is not so. Discipline is defined as teaching your child what to *do* as well as what *not* to do. This is not to say you should use discipline to shape your child into what you want your child to be but rather to help your child achieve their potential and become the unique individual they were meant to be (Ashston and Ashston 1996). We need to start right now and teach you how to discipline your child and clear up your misconceptions. Viewing discipline as something we all live with on a day-to-day basis may make it easier for you to carry out your responsibilities. We are either well-disciplined people or we're not. If we have been well disciplined as children, then usually we become self-disciplined adults. If, on the other hand, we have not been well disciplined then life becomes a chore and we continue to need discipline from others because we are incapable of providing discipline for ourselves.

If children do not get a clear message from the adults in their environments regarding what is right and what is wrong, then children will seek out others to help answer the questions they have about good and bad, right and wrong, appropriate and inappropriate. Unfortunately, the individuals they most often seek out generally have the same lifetime experiences they do and usually are close to the same age. These individuals are their peers. So, peer groups become a greater influence on these children than the adults in their environment.

Technology is another source of influence for children. If children are left at home to care for themselves, they may make the decision to watch television programs that aren't appropriate for them or to get on unsupervised Internet chat rooms. In some cases this technology becomes a greater influence than the parents themselves. So between the peer group and the technology, you have significant competition in rearing your child. Parents must take an active role in attending to these challenges or the result is likely to be a child who is poorly disciplined and who will suffer from the consequences of this lack of guidance.

Making You a Strong Parent

So often parents wonder why they can't get their kids to behave. Much of the time they have not looked at themselves and the baggage they bring to the relationship. The saying "actions speak louder than words" is applicable here. If a parent is having trouble dealing with their own problems such as obesity, marital problems, alcoholism, anger control, depression, or poor self-esteem, to mention just a few, often children react by either worrying about them or failing to respect them. The worst-case scenario in this situation is that little effort on either parent's behalf is put into the child's upbringing. Then your child does not look to you for guidance and discipline but to their peer group or other sources.

Caring for Yourself

It seems like common sense that if you take care of yourself, you will have more stamina and energy to rear your child. A parent who does not attend to their own needs has minimal reserves to put toward the most important job of their life. You need to take care of yourself for the following things:

- Physical problems

- Emotional problems

- Self-esteem problems

- Communication problems

- Career problems

Perhaps you are wondering what this has to do with disciplining your child. Many times parents say to me, "I am not here for me. My problems and past have nothing to do with how my child misbehaves. The child needs the help, not me." These are common responses when one tries to look at their problems. I can guarantee you that if you don't take care of your own problems then you only need to look into the mirror to see why you are having so many problems with your child.

Lets look at ways to take care of yourself so that you can take care of your child. It may be hard for you to do this but it must start with you.

Physical Condition

When parents do not have the energy to carry out the responsibilities of parenting they need to look at their own physical condition. What is your weight? If you happen to be overweight you may not have the energy to keep up with your child. Should it surprise you that being overweight may lead to blood pressure problems, heart problems, type 2 diabetes, and joint problems, to name just a few? You probably need to see your doctor to determine if there is a reason for your weight gain and lack of energy. Contrary to most people's opinion, weight gain is most likely not due to glandular problems (like one wants to believe) but due to the lack of exercise and overeating. Lack of exercise may lead to being overweight and to any fatigue that you're experiencing. I am never surprised to see the offspring of heavy parents be heavy as well, which is another good reason to address the problem.

Other eating problems that I see in parents that tend to be seen in their children are those that end up with significant weight loss. Many times bulimia and anorexia are lifelong problems and you will have to get help for them throughout your entire life. You are your child's role model. Model healthy eating and exercise habits.

If you happen to be a parent who suffers from some type of chronic illness, make sure you have adequate medical care so that you can manage your illness and monitor the status of your condition. Also make sure you adhere to the medical regimen you have been placed on. If you don't feel your health is as good as it should be, check with your doctor. You may need a second opinion to make sure everything is being done for you. A sick parent has very little energy to put towards taking care of their child, and what happens all too often is the child ends up taking care of you rather than the opposite. This overwhelming sense of responsibility can be a factor in the child's depression, so it's best to try to take care of the problem yourself.

If by chance you don't have any of the aforementioned conditions but you just don't feel good, go to your doctor. It's important to find the cause for not feeling good so that you feel like getting up in the morning and carrying out your responsibilities as a parent. It also might help you to enjoy life for yourself, too. Remember, if you are not enjoying life then you are not going to have the energy to enjoy your children.

Emotional Problems

I commonly see parents who are suffering from their own emotional distresses. I have parents who are so depressed that they don't have the energy to get through a day taking care of themselves, much less their children. If you are carrying some baggage from your own childhood or if you have other emotional issues going on in your life that you've never addressed with a professional, I would recommend that you do so as soon as possible. Your children detect the depression or anxiety you are experiencing and in some instances may begin to experience some of the same feelings. Also, children don't understand why they have to seek help for their behavior problems when their parents don't get help for their own problems. Frequently I hear, "I don't have the problem, my parents do." Kids who say this may be right, or it may be that both of you have emotional problems. All too often children worry that they are going to have problems like Mom, Dad, or even that cousin who tried to commit suicide. You may share the same concerns and wonder if your child's behavior changes are the first sign that they are getting the "family illness." Your child, on the other hand, may hesitate to disclose how they are really feeling because they're afraid you'll think they're just like that family member who went "off the deep end." Getting help for yourself may give your child permission to open up and ask for help. The message you're sending is, there is help, and you don't have to end up like your relative.

You may come from a background where anger was the way to communicate and that is how you handle your stress; if so, try getting help for this, too. Children stop communicating with their parents if every time they say or do something they get an angry response. Children feel like they are walking on eggshells if they are never sure what will provoke your anger. You will begin to see the anger in return, and you'll wonder where it came from. Take a look at yourself.

The other problem I see with parents is that they are unwilling to address their smoking or their problems with alcoholism or drugs. The myriad of problems associated with these addictions is beyond the scope of this book, but remember that your addiction issues need to be addressed or you might be looking at the same problems with your child. A word of warning—don't role model your vices for your child. The message your child takes from this information is if it's okay for my parent, it's okay for me. Your child will challenge you the first time you catch them experimenting with tobacco, alcohol, or drugs. This will not be a challenge you will be able to defend.

If marital problems are a source of problems for you and your spouse, get help. Parents often will tell me that their children don't know that they are having problems. I just can't buy that. Don't you all live in the same house? If you think that your arguments go unheard, then you'd better think again. You cannot insulate your doors and walls enough so that your children don't hear your "discussions." Besides, who knows your behaviors any better than the child you brought into the world? They will pick up on your distress immediately. Many times a child I'm seeing will quote to me verbatim from the discussion their parents had the night before while their parent tries to tell me that their child does not have a clue that there are marital problems. If either mental or physical abuse is occurring, the child will also be aware of it. They may even feel responsible for the parent that is being abused and feel they can't leave their parents alone or something quite bad will happen. In some instances one or both parents do blame the child for their problems. In this and all cases of abuse, you'd better have a professional help you sort through the problem.

When there is trouble in your marriage your child may worry about one parent to the extent that they feel they need to protect that parent. What that child needs to see is that you get help for your problem so that they'll learn that it's not okay to be a victim. Your child needs to realize that these problems are yours and your spouse's and not their own. They must know that your marriage is your responsibility and that in no way are they responsible for your problems. So get help and quit talking, discussing, and fighting behind closed doors. Remember, the doors might as well be open.

Self-Esteem Problems

Self-esteem is defined as a way of thinking and looking at yourself that implies that you appreciate yourself, believe in yourself, and trust your own self-worth. If you do not have a feeling of self-worth, then life is going to be very lonely and very painful for you. Parents with low self-esteem have very little faith in what they think they can do for and with their families. Their children pick up on the uneasiness their parents have with disciplining them and often respond by testing their parents more in an attempt to get some order in their lives. These children usually get inconsistent discipline and many times the discipline becomes a shouting match.

Parents with self-esteem issues come to me because they recognize they are losing control of their children. They brought their low self-esteem to their marriage and parenting, and their self-esteem has become worse because they do not seem to have the parenting successes that would reinforce them and give them the message that they are good parents.

A parent's low self-esteem is not something that just suddenly occurs when they get married and have their first baby. Often a parent's self-esteem is determined by his or her own childhood and adolescent experiences. What you have learned while growing up usually determines what you bring to your marriage and to your children. If you were abused, you may bring abuse to these new relationships, or you may marry into an abusive situation. In other instances you may decide that you will do everything you can to not be abusive toward your children and then go to the other extreme and not discipline your children. The end result is that you are strict and your child is not allowed to do anything at all outside the home. Or you become very lenient because somehow you equate discipline and abuse. Your parents may have perpetrated physical abuse under the guise of discipline.

Clearly, you need to understand that abuse can be physical, verbal, or sexual, or due to neglect, and is directly linked to your self-esteem. It may be the result of your low self-esteem or it may contribute to your low self-esteem. Abuse is never a good thing for you and your children and must be addressed with a professional in every situation in which it is occurring. If you choose not to get help then you can be assured that your children will suffer from what is going on, even if they are not the direct victims of the abuse. Your child's self-esteem and the degree of respect they have for themselves is a mirror of what you have communicated to them by your reactions to your own abuse.

Communication Problems

You learned your methods and style of communication with others in part from the way you were reared by your parents and other people in your environment. They were the role models for you on how to communicate with your spouse, your children, the members of your extended family, your friends, and people in various roles in society. You may have had parents who always listened to you, displayed appropriate concern, reflected on how they thought you were feeling, and always had time for you. Or just the opposite, you may have had parents that were more negative, rarely listened to you, displayed anger all the time, were very moody, and may have been abusive. No matter what your past was like, it will most likely influence how you will approach your parenting role.

If you were taught that your parents never had time to listen then you are likely to have trouble finding time for your children. If you were reared in a household of criticism, then you most likely will criticize, and if you were reared by angry parents, you will probably rear your child as an angry parent. These are only a few examples of how your parent's ways of parenting you will likely influence how you will parent your children. If those ways you parent tend to result from a more negative upbringing of your own, you may want to be very careful that you don't overlook your own needs. In other words, you need to get help and guidance to break the negative child rearing cycles of your past.

You might be asking why your problems need to be looked at when your child has the problem. If your child is struggling, this trouble may be from a number of reasons but one important consideration is your behavior as a parent. If you are a parent who communicates in a warm, affectionate, positive, and playful manner, you are more likely to see more positive child-parent interactions, improved child compliance, and improved satisfaction with your parenting role and your marriage relationship in your family (Dix 1991; Howard 1996).

Career Problems

Children worry about adults' problems and usually this is their parents' problems. In my practice I've found that if it is not their parents' marriage they are worried about, it's their parents' financial problems. All too often this stems from parents being laid off, being fired, or being demoted. In other instances parents simply cannot find work that can support their family. So often this seems to occur after a divorce when usually the mother is trying to rear the children, get them to school, and find after-school care, while holding a job. This job has to be conducive to these time constraints as well as one that can support the expense of child care and the household. The life events that result from this often create a very stressful environment for all members of the family. Why should it surprise us that the children worry about their parent's jobs and the financial security of their family?

These are the kinds of stressors that parents bring to child rearing. There may be times in your life when you feel you need some professional help for these stressors. It's okay to get that help. You might find that this type of support will help you feel you are capable of handling your child's everyday behavior and their troubled behavior. Child rearing is a challenge and needs to be done by parents who feel like they have control of their own lives.

Effective Discipline

Now that we've covered the basics of what discipline is and what the parent can do for themselves to improve discipline in the house, we're ready to discuss how good discipline is achieved. First of all, it's important to understand that nowhere is knowing basic behavioral principles more important than when providing discipline for your child. Keep in mind that discipline is teaching your child with the aim of helping your child "achieve competence, self control, and self direction" (Howard 1996). I tell parents that if they doubt the importance of discipline then they want to think how brokenhearted they will be if their child is always left out of school activities such as birthday parties or sleepovers because they are seen by parents, teachers, and other children as the class behavior problem. Teachers and coaches will see your child as a nuisance and so your child misses out on some school activities or sits on the sidelines while classmates participate in a team sport.

Basic Rules

In order to help your child be accepted by their peers and the adults in their environment there are some rules to consider before learning the actual discipline techniques we're going to examine.

Recognize the good things about your child. First and foremost, remember to recognize the good behavior your child is demonstrating and their accomplishments. Behavioral psychologists refer to this opportunity as "catch them being good." If you don't take this opportunity and find yourself dwelling on only those times the child is bad then I can guarantee you the number of bad acts will increase. If, on the other hand, you praise your child for their appropriate behavior and describe the behavior to them, it's likely that they will learn from this and continue with good behavior. There are times when this recognition should be done in the form of touch without verbal feedback. This is especially nice when your child is concentrating on some activity that requires their full attention. A touch lets them know you are giving them feedback for their behavior and at the same time you are not interrupting their focus on the project. It makes sense to use touch as much as possible during quiet times so that their attention span is reinforced. Catch your child when they are good and you will promote more good behavior.

The punishment needs to fit the crime. One of the biggest errors I see in parenting is that parents punish their child excessively for the infraction that has occurred. Children come to me feeling like no matter what they do they will be grounded for an excessive amount of time (for instance, grounding for a month for forgetting to call home). The other common thing parents do is take away all of the their child's toys without any incentive to earn them back. And finally, it is not uncommon that a child misbehaves at school and the school disciplines them and then notifies the parents—who discipline them again. It's easy to understand that this sort of double punishment could really hurt a kid's sense of self-esteem.

Use manners in your home. Parents who don't use "please" and "thank you" to all family members can expect the same from their child. A home where good manners are not used and respect is not had by all is a home that teaches the same behavior to their children for in and outside the home. A child without manners and one who is disrespectful to others, both young and old, will soon be considered a rude and uncaring person. The result may be a very lonely child—people do not like to be around rude people.

Make rules very clear. The rules in your home need to be clear and consistently implemented. This may require you to write them out at times. If rules aren't clear, your child may not know what to anticipate and may be anxious that they will inadvertently displease you. Usually, a child's major goal in life is to please their parents.

Be consistent with your child. If your child never knows what will tick you off and what is expected of them, then they live in fear that your wrath may come down at any time. It's important that the child can anticipate the same reaction from you for the same infraction of the rule each time it happens. Otherwise, the insecurity of their position can really contribute to their depression.

Don't discuss things when you're angry. No matter how badly you want to discuss with your child what they've done wrong, it's always best to wait until everyone has cooled down. First, if you are angry you will most likely go on and on about what is bothering you. You will probably become even angrier as you get into your reprimands. And if your child is angry as well, they will probably become angrier in response to your verbal attacks. You both may end up saying things you don't mean. You are also likely to misunderstand each other, and so what could have been a civil discussion tends to escalate to a heated argument. Saying and hearing these sorts of negative things may end up hurting your child's self-esteem and really doesn't do much good for yours, either.

Recognize that children will misbehave. Try to remember that it's normal for children to misbehave and that a normal and natural response is parental anger. Expressing a lot of anger is not necessary in order to get your child's attention, nor is anger needed for disciplining. When a parent tells me that they just can't stand their child's behavior anymore, I remind them that they have been standing it, in some instances for many years, and reassure them that they will be able to continue to stand it until they learn some discipline techniques. It's also important to remember that even if parents are outstanding disciplinarians, there will be times when their child will misbehave. Misbehavior is one way a child learns, and it doesn't reflect on your adequacy as a parent.

See yourself as a role model. Parents often forget that their children learn how to behave by watching them. If you tend to scream and cuss, you can probably expect your child to do the same thing. If you drink and use drugs, your child will likely be at high risk for this self-destructive behavior, too. If they see you lying for them to get them out of school or they see you lying to someone to get yourself out of something, then they will think it's okay for them to lie as well. The basic message is that your children are what you are.

Always listen to your child. Children generally have a time of day that they like to talk and share with their parents. If this time doesn't fit into your schedule and you don't sit down and listen to what your child has to say, you're going to miss some very important information about your child. Another great time to keep your ears open is when you find yourself driving your child and their friends around. It can be like you are not even there. Also, if you are the carpool parent, it's a great time to pick up on what is happening with your children and their peers. The message here is take the time to listen to your child.

Speak calmly. Far too often parents seem to think that yelling at their child gets their attention more. If you're truly trying to communicate with your child, and not simply demonstrating that you're angry, you'll need to use a calm, normal tone of voice. That way, there is less likelihood that your interaction will result in a major meltdown. Additionally, the message you give to your child is that you feel badly about the way things have worked out but they still have to do what you ask them to do. As an example, think of yourself in your work setting. If your superiors yelled at you all the time, you would probably quit. It just doesn't make for a productive environment. I remind my patients' parents that if I yelled at them they would get up and leave and think I was some type of nutcase. Yelling and being very stern will not end up obtaining the cooperation of your child. It also is not good for your child's self-esteem, and it's probably not good for your self-esteem either.

Another one of my pet peeves is when parents don't inform their children about important things that are going on in their family and the child hears about it from friends or the parents of friends. This is a sure way to alienate your child and make them feel unimportant. I can remember working with a child who had to learn her family was moving from her best friend. The girl's mother had told this best friend's mother, but not her own child. Boy, is that a way to hurt the trust you've built with your child. This problem is far more common than you might think and it does more damage than you might assume. Don't become part of the problem.

If your child confides in you, be sure you're not sharing their confidences with your child's friends' parents. To confide means for your child to show trust in you by sharing intimate secrets.

Once you disclose these secrets to someone else, it will eventually get back to your child even if you don't think it will. It always does. Then you've done damage to the trust you share with your child. Trust is the foundation for a good relationship with your child, and now the foundation is cracked. It is unlikely that your child will share any more of their secrets. Do both of you a favor and respect your child's need for privacy.

Have family meals. Families need time together after their busy days and they've traditionally found that time at dinnertime. It is a time that all members of the family can share what has been happening and what is concerning them. You will also discover if your child's eating habits have changed, which may indicate they are either ill or very stressed. Eating is together time, sharing time, and observation time.

Take time for your children's activities. All too often parents are so overextended that they feel they don't have the time, energy, or desire to be involved in their child's activities. But as a parent your job is to be involved, and once you reorganize your time to include them, you might find that your child and their peers will actually energize you. Hanging out with them is also a good way to get to know your child's friends and their parents. This is essential for knowing whom your child is hanging out with and what kind of supervision they will be having when they are at their friends' homes. Involvement in their activities shows your children you care and sends the message to others involved that you care about and support your child.

Get involved in your child's home responsibilities. First of all, your child does need to have chores at home that they are responsible for, but the assignment of these chores needs to be reasonable. Unfortunately, some parents use their children as their housekeepers. Keeping up your home is a family project, not your kid's project. For instance, if you ask your child to clean a room, dig in and help. It's a great way to show your child you're willing to do your part, and it's a wonderful opportunity to "catch them being good."

Spend more time with your children than you do with your friends. Sometimes parents think that because they work so hard, they have the right to take the whole weekend for their own pleasure, leaving very little time for their kids. Keep in mind that your child did not ask to come into this world—that was a choice you made. Now you have the responsibility to participate in their activities. If you feel that your own bucket is empty and you need time for yourself then try to work it out with your child's other parent so that you can take turns and you can have some time to rejuvenate yourself. But children need to know that their parents care, and they will know that if you spend time with them. So make a point to spend more time with your kids than knocking around with your friends.

Be a part of your child's school and extracurricular activities. There is no better way to know your kid's teacher and classmates than to be involved in school and athletic activities. If there is a need for a room mother or a coach or a chaperone, then do it. If you are a working parent and don't have daytime hours to be involved, then ask if there are some other things you can do on an occasional evening. Don't be surprised when they say "yes."

Spend time reading and playing with your child. Take the time to read with your child on a daily basis. This allows you to be close to them while advancing your child's reading skills and vocabulary. Board games are also an important way of spending time with your child. They allow you numerous opportunities to give your child feedback on good things they are doing and give you time to just have fun together. Families can spend genuine play time together to get to know each other and to teach the child appropriate competitive behavior. Playing together also teaches your child that some games are for the fun of it and that you don't have to be a winner each time. This is a lesson that is rarely taught in our sports programs today.

Don't give your child everything they want. Lots of children feel very entitled today. They can become distraught if they can't have something they want, and many times they're not willing to work for it. Children need to be taught that one must earn what one wants, whether it's toys or good grades. What they need to know is that they don't have to earn the love and attention of their parents. Children today feel like they have to earn love and attention and that they deserve material goods. I think you'll agree that this is an awful message to send to your child.

Say you're sorry if you have offended your child. Parents sometimes believe that, because they are the parent, they don't have to or shouldn't apologize when they make a mistake. Perhaps they feel that their authority will be undermined if they're ever seen as wrong, but not being honest will only hurt the respect their child has for them. Children never forget those instances where they legitimately feel that a parent owes them an apology and they don't get it. After all, respect is a two-way street. They will take the memory of the incident into adulthood. Hopefully the lesson they have learned is to not carry on the tradition of not apologizing.

Don't embarrass your child. It is highly important that you become sensitive to your child and watch that your corrections are not in front of their peers or in public. Although there are times when your child may need to have feedback on the way they are treating a friend who is visiting or the way they are acting in public, you can offer that feedback so that it is not done in the public's eye or in front of the friend. Friends may not want to play with your child if they are always put in the position of witnessing an altercation between your child and you. It becomes uncomfortable for all parties, and human beings avoid what is uncomfortable for them. Besides, your child may begin to mistrust your behavior when they have friends over. So it may be just one more thing to undermine your child's trust in you.

Discipline Is Rooted in Behavior

As you begin to read this section, you may wonder why I have stressed that discipline is so important for depressed children. In my experience, I have learned that depressed children are often allowed to be too much in control of their own lives. This certainly is not because their parents don't care, but because their parents are cutting them a ton of slack. So often parents feel guilty that their child isn't doing well and end up believing that if they give their child fewer responsibilities and more control over their own lives that their child's irritability will somehow magically disappear. You will discover, however, the contrary will be true. All children, and especially those who are struggling, need effective, firm, and consistent discipline. So let's check out ways to help you provide this.

First, let's look at some behavior principles that I want you to be familiar with so that when we look at how to discipline your child you will know that the rules I suggest are based on what works from a behavioral standpoint.

Grandma's Rule

This stands for the idea that you must work before you play. That way, play can then act as a reinforcer (Becker 1971). For instance, if a child wants to play on their computer when they get home from school, you might require that they do their homework first. When they finish that, they can then play on the computer.

Consequence

This is the term used to describe what happens after a response to something. If a rewarding consequence follows a response, then it is likely to increase the likelihood of that same thing happening again. If the consequence is a punishment, then it will decrease the likelihood of that happening again. There are times that you might think that you have punished your child when in fact just the opposite has occurred. Let's look at an example of this.

For example, let's say that you're on the phone and your eight-year-old begins teasing their sister to the point that you can't hear what the other person is saying. You get off the phone and reprimand your child for teasing their sister. Later that day you are on the phone and the same scenario happens. Why would the child do the same thing again when you just reprimanded them? Well, notice that your child has gotten your attention even if it is a reprimand. That's better than no attention at all, which they perceived was happening when you were on the phone. In this case, the reprimand is the consequence to your child teasing their sister and interrupting your phone conversation. You might think that the reprimand is a punishment, but it actually rewards your child. They are getting your attention and have found that it works every time. In other words, the behavior has been positively reinforced. Consequences can be tricky like that sometimes.

Reinforcement

Reinforcement is what immediately follows a response and that increases the likelihood of that response occurring again. In order for it to be a positive reinforcement the response must increase in frequency, duration, or intensity.

To illustrate, let's say there is a child who has been told that if they study their spelling words each day without a reminder, they will get fifty cents right after they finish. So each time the child studies spelling words they earn fifty cents. With a deal like that, the child begins studying their spelling words and they earn money every day. The child has been positively reinforced for studying without a parent reminding them.

Punishment

Punishment is one kind of consequence that follows a response. It's intended to decrease or eliminate the response that it follows. It can consist of the removal of positive reinforcement, which is also known as "extinction." Ignoring a negative behavior is an example of this type of punishment. Another form of punishment is an aversive event that follows a response. Corporal punishment, reprimands, and negative facial responses are considered to be this type of punishment. Punishment should not be the first approach to changing a behavior of a child.

As I mentioned above, ignoring a behavior can be a form of punishment. "Planned ignoring" is ignoring a behavior either by looking away, walking away, or changing the topic of a conversation (Hall and Hall 1980). As soon as the behavior changes to something more appropriate, then you would focus your attention on the more positive behavior. For instance, let's say your child is complaining about their sister taking too long in the bathroom. The child runs to you yelling, "She's an idiot!" This seems to happen every morning and you are tired of hearing the complaint. This time you have planned to turn and walk away from the child and begin talking to their father about some topic in the news. Initially the child gets even more angry, but you continue to ignore their angry behavior. Finally your child calms down and says they need to get into the bathroom in a nice tone. You immediately pay attention and go to see if you can speed up the other child or open up your bathroom for use.

Another punishment, which I do not condone, is hitting your kid. This type of punishment is usually an impulsive response, though in some situations spanking is more planned. Hitting is most often counterproductive because it may result in your child becoming angrier. I also caution you that if you are doing the spanking, you may get carried away with your own anger, which would ultimately result in abuse of the child.

Reinforcers

Reinforcers are those natural interaction behaviors you display towards your child such as touch, a hug, praise, attention, and smiling. These are learned reinforcers and should be used by you immediately after the child engages in an appropriate behavior. Researchers refer to this as "time-in" (Christophersen 2002) and it is used either alone or in combination with time-out. It is also referred to by behaviorists as "catching them being good."

Token reinforcers are symbols of reinforcers, such as chips, points, or stickers. In the adult world, money earned is a token reinforcer. These reinforcers must be given immediately after the target behavior has occurred. After a certain preestablished number of tokens have been earned they can be exchanged for a backup reinforcer such as a specific treat, TV minutes, or computer minutes.

Applications in Discipline

When parents bring their child in to my office because they see the child acting out and refusing to do what they ask, the most important thing I do after a thorough assessment is made is to help the parents gain control of the situation. I'm always glad they've come to me for help because it's important to provide discipline based on research and not some arbitrarily determined approach that your neighbor has suggested. Many times, depressed kids will test the adults in their lives to see who is in control. Your effective discipline should send them the message that you're the one in charge.

Initially, you do not want to start with punishment, which is really what many parents want to do because they are so desperate to gain control. But if you don't start with punishment, where do you start? Lets look at the role that positive reinforcement plays.

Using Positive Reinforcement

Starting with positive reinforcement can help keep things light, letting you avoid the role of harsh disciplinarian. Remember, positive reinforcement is rewarding good behavior in order to encourage more of it. Here are some specific techniques to help you apply this understanding to the situations you're facing.

Time-in. You start with identifying the appropriate behavior that is displayed by your child. In other words you catch them being good. This means you give your attention to your child for the appropriate behavior your child displays. This is more than saying, "Good job, Sandy," but rather describing to Sandy what she is doing that warrants your attention. So let's say Sandy picked up her book bag and put it in her closet without being asked. As soon as she does it, you would say "Thank you for picking up your book bag and putting it in your closet." Acknowledging this positive behavior immediately after it happens will reinforce it and result in a greater likelihood of the behavior occurring again. Makes sense, doesn't it, when you consider the rule of reinforcement?

Another very important way to provide time-in or positive feedback is through touch without using words. What—no words? Yes! Lets say, for instance, that your son George is doing his homework, a thing he has not done much in the past. You like to go check on him. Initially, you went every three to five minutes to check on him and asked how he was doing. Each time he would stop his work and want to talk to you or want you to stay to help him. Later your psychologist advised you just to go into his room and pat him on the shoulder and then walk out. You started doing this at short time intervals, then you stretched out the interval but never made the interval the same. Two things were going on that were good. First, you didn't talk so you could avoid interrupting him at the very thing you were trying to reinforce, studying and focusing. Second, you checked on him at different time intervals, which helps maintain the target behavior more than if he knows when you're going to check on him.

Another thing time-in is used for is to give feedback for the appropriate behavior. This is so that the amount of appropriate behavior will increase over time. Sometimes parents don't think their child has any good behavior. I want to stress that all children display appropriate behavior, even if you don't think so. If you have a hard time identifying good behavior then try describing to yourself or to the other parent one inappropriate behavior you want your child to change. Then describe what it would look like if it were an appropriate behavior. Have you taught your child in clear terms what you want them to do? If not, see that you do, and have them practice it. Now, instead of always pointing out to your child when they display the inappropriate behavior, you should instead ignore it. That means don't comment on it, don't look at them, and if you can, walk away. Then, when they perform the appropriate behavior, attend to them immediately and point the good behavior out either by verbal feedback, with a touch, or with a hug.

Lets say Johnny baby talks every time he wants a snack. You don't like the baby talk, but in your mind the only way to get him to stop is to give him the snack. He is now nine years old and you think he's too old for baby talk. You decide that you will first clearly let him know that you want him to ask in more mature language if he wants a snack. You demonstrate how he should ask for the snack. Then you have him return the demonstration. He understands what you expect of him. The next time, he proceeds to baby talk when he wants some chips and dip. This time you walk away and begin talking to his sibling. He subsequently changes and asks in a more mature manner, "Mother, may I have some chips and dip?" This time you give him his snack and tell him you appreciate the way he asked you. Now, your temptation may be to provide him a long speech on why he did such a good job and why he did not get it the first time he asked. Please don't do this. You have already taught him his lesson. Short, sweet lessons are important. Remember, if he reverts back to his baby talk, ignore it and reinforce him when he asks in a more mature way. He is a child and sometimes it takes a few trials and errors to get on board with the program.

Time-out. Ignoring is a form of time-out. This means that in order to give a child a time-out, you don't always have to put them in a time-out chair. When parents tell me time-out is not working, I've found that they are most likely not giving enough positive feedback to their child. If this is in the deficit, then your child will misbehave to get attention even if it means giving them a time-out in a chair. Punishment is attention, and if the child is not getting enough attention then provoking punishment will be their way of getting attention.

As long as we are talking about time-out, I want to make sure you're very clear on what it is. Time-out is an extreme form of ignoring in which the child is removed from all attention or the attention is removed from them. The child can be placed in time-out in a chair, on a step, on a park bench, in a room, and so forth. I personally don't think you should have only one chair in your house where they always spend time-out, because it seems to happen that if the child misbehaves in another part of the house, you may not give them a time-out because it is too much trouble to take them to another part of the house where the time-out chair is. Typically, the child is sent to time-out for one minute per year of age, up to five minutes. The catch is, they have to be quiet for the length of the time-out. If they continue to act out in spite of having been in time-out for five minutes, they don't get out until they've been quiet for five minutes. This teaches them self-control. It also is a cooling-down period if they are angry. If you tell the child they can come out of time-out and they refuse, you then just reset the timer. You never want them to determine when they come out. That is your job. You are the parent, and you tell them when they can come out of time-out from a chair, their room, or any other designated area. Obviously if the child is quiet and cooperative then they have chosen to behave and have taken control of themselves, and this should result in their getting out. Remember, time-out places a child in a situation where they won't get *any* attention for inappropriate behavior. Also remember that when your child says this is a stupid way of disciplining and it doesn't work, you should have a pretty good idea then that it *is* starting to work. One more word about time-out is, if it's truly not working, then one or both of the following things must be considered. Either there is something else going on with your child that has not been diagnosed or you're not using time-out in the correct way. Remember, there should be much more positive feedback for appropriate behavior than time-out, or any other punishment for that matter.

Token systems. Barkley (1996a) refers to a token system as an "essential prosthetic device" for correcting a child's behavior. Some children find it hard to do what's expected of them, while some parents find it difficult to find positive things about their child to reinforce. The token system is a way of helping both in these situations.

Setting up a token system can be difficult if you're not sure how to go about doing it. It has to be done in detail and with the help and cooperation of both parents and the child. I'd like to stress that if you don't think you have the time to set it up properly or carry it out, then you might want to wait before doing it. Also, if after you read the explanation here, you're still not totally clear about how to set up the system, you should seek the advice of a mental-health professional or a teacher who is familiar with how to do it.

Tokens can be poker chips, colored paper cut into equal-sized squares, or points, though points are usually used with older children. The goal is to be able to give your child *frequent* and *immediate* feedback for the task they have performed or the rule they have followed. Remember, immediate positive feedback is key for initiating, increasing, and maintaining a behavior. Also remember that a token alone would only be reinforcement for a short while. It would be like you having no ability to spend your money on anything because it's not worth anything but the way it looks and feels in your pocket. You might stop working for a paycheck if it could not be cashed in for anything. Unless of course you have a lot of intrinsic motivation, your money needs to be able to buy things. We all need feedback and it is best to get it immediately.

So, in summary, a token system is a method to provide your child a symbolic reinforcement (like chips or points) that can be exchanged later for real reinforcement (like TV time). A point system is a type of token system. To set up a token system, go through the following steps:

- **Select the token.** You and your child should pick a token that they prefer. If a point system (Christophersen 1994) is used, make sure your child can tally up how many points they have earned and spent each day. Usually a school-age child prefers points. If you do use points, make sure you make a tally sheet where you add and subtract what has been earned versus what has been spent.

- **Make a list of backup reinforcers.** Identify a list of backup reinforcers that your child can buy with their earned tokens. I like to do this early so your child sees the program as something to reinforce them, not to punish them. The reinforcers should be daily privileges such as TV time, computer time, and play time. There may also be privileges that are more special and can be bought at the end of a week or at a later time. Usually these will cost quite a bit more, and your child will have to save up extra tokens in their savings account to be able to exchange them for these more special privileges.

Don't make them impossible to earn. These privileges might include things such as a movie, a special meal, or a trip to an amusement park. This list of backup reinforcers should be generated with the help of your child. If they have siblings, it may be a good idea to initially put all of them on the system, just as it is important to base all of your discipline for all of your children on behavioral principles. Also, remember to leave some pleasurable activities off the list. Some things, such as their meals, a bedtime story, or playing catch with Dad are the sorts of activities that should be given freely. Requiring everything to be bought may end up with your child having a very negative reaction to your new approach to discipline. Remember, this is not to punish your child but to encourage them.

• **Write down the chores and rules.** To start off, you must write down the chores and rules in order to avoid any confusion between you and your child. You might be feeling stretched for time, so you verbally agree with your child that they must do certain chores in order to earn a specific number of tokens. However, this will likely get you both into trouble. Rules and chores have a way of changing when they haven't been defined. Both the chores and the rules must be written out. If rules and chores are clearly stated in writing, then there will be no misunderstanding about what is expected of your child. You may want to consider posting this list, if it's feasible. Otherwise it should be placed where you both have access to it.

• **Write down what behaviors earn.** Once the behaviors have been identified, then you must specify how many tokens are earned for each behavior and write that on the list. The amounts earned should vary with age and individual circumstances. For example, lower amounts might be given for the younger child and their simpler tasks, whereas older children can earn more for their more-complex tasks. For example, an eight-year-old may earn five to twenty-five points for doing their chore and a ten-year-old may earn in the range of twenty-five to one hundred points for what they do. This way, the older child can have their more complex chores broken down and are then paid every few minutes rather than at the completion of a chore (Barkley 1996a). Also, more points can be given to a child who is more resistant to doing a chore. How much you pay can be revised, so keep in mind none of this is etched in stone. What is earned needs to be paid immediately, to get the benefit of immediate reinforcement. Don't put off payment, or the whole reason for the point system will be undermined.

Here's an example of what a small list might look like.

> Makes bed, including neatly pulling up sheets and bedspread—earns five points.
>
> Empties the dishwasher and puts dishes away—earns five points.
>
> Dusts each piece of furniture in the family room—earns 10 points.

* **Use the two-thirds rule.** Figure out how much your child is likely to earn each day. Then, when you're figuring out what they need to spend for privileges, make sure it is about two-thirds of what they earn each day (Barkley 1996a). Make sure that they don't spend everything on one privilege. The leftover points or tokens are then put in a savings account for the bigger privileges that can be earned later in the week. However, it's very important that your child gets plenty of opportunities to spend their tokens on privileges on the day that they earn the tokens. If you always wait until the end of the week, your token system won't work because the reinforcement is not being given immediately. So to reiterate, make sure your child earns tokens immediately and has the opportunity to spend them on the day they earn them. Also, give your child the chance to save for something bigger at the end of the week.

* **Use bonus tokens.** When you start a token system, make
  sure your child receives several bonuses for good behavior that's not necessarily on the list, things such as coop-
  erating, eye contact, and good manners. This should be
  done from the moment you give them their first tokens.

Here's an example of how this might work. Let's say that
Jane's mother asked her to put her book bag away. Not only
could Jane earn the designated points for performing this task but
she might earn bonus points because she said "thank you" to her
mother when her mother actually gave her the points. This thank
you was not specified to earn points on the written rules—it
would be just a little added benefit.

* **Stick with positives first.** As you know, it's important to
  give positive feedback a chance before you jump to
  punishment. I can assure you that if punishment is
  started too early, there will be no incentive for your child
  to want to use the token program. Start the token
  program off with only positive feedback in the form of
  tokens. Use positives for the first two weeks and then
  start taking away tokens if their behavior warrants.
  Remember, your job is to encourage your child. Also
  make sure that when you do start fining your child that
  you remember that they should be given two times more
  tokens than are being taken away. Also it's important
  that the same number of tokens are taken away as are
  given for the same chore. In the event that your child
  doesn't comply even after being fined, send them to
  time-out. After a successful completion of a time-out, let
  them earn some bonus tokens when they return. This is a
  nice way to remain positive in spite of their not comply-
  ing earlier.

* **Getting off a token system.** A child can be given the
  incentive to earn their way off of the token system. Give
  them a predetermined number of points that they'll need
  to pay to get off the system. This should be a significant
  number, and I would suggest that this should only be
  after six to eight weeks of being on it. When the token
  system is gone, the child is still required to behave or do
  their chores when you ask them once. If their compliance
  remains a problem, then they need to go back on the

system. Your child needs to know that you are the one in charge of whether they go back on it. The only say they have in this is by making the choice to behave.

Now take a look at David's story at the beginning of this chapter. From what you've learned, can you see how you would help David's mother and father? Really, don't you think David is asking for someone to take charge of him? It must be scary for a school-age child, or any child for that matter, to feel like they are in charge and that it doesn't matter what they do. No wonder David is so irritable with his parents and his mother is so tired. Both parents in this case need some professional guidance so that they can work together for the sake of the child. Parenting without anger and parenting as a team are essential.

Summary

We've been looking at common-sense rules regarding child rearing and at the specific behavioral principles you need to consider when you discipline your child. I'd like you to take from this chapter the idea that discipline is teaching the child to have self-discipline with the aim of them being a very productive person in society. You've learned the importance of eliminating anger from your discipline, focusing on the child's positives, and giving the child feedback about these positives. Parents need to always bear in mind that they are role models for their children. If the child does not respect the role models in their home then they will begin searching outside the home.

The child with depression who is exhibiting acting-out behavior clearly is telling us they are out of control. Addressing these control issues is the parents' challenge. The first step to this challenge is providing consistent, effective, and loving discipline.

In the next chapter you'll learn about the concepts of cognitive interventions, relaxation exercises, and visual imagery. These, along with what you have learned about discipline, can be combined to help your child feel more hopeful about today and tomorrow.

Chapter 6

Your Child Needs to Learn to Think Positively

∞ *Brenda's Story*

Brenda came home the Friday afternoon of her first week back at school and screamed at her mother, "My teacher is so mean, I hate her." Her mother held Brenda in her arms while the girl sobbed. Her mother tried to reassure her that although her teacher seemed mean to her, she was probably having a bad day. "Besides" she added, "some years you just have mean teachers." Her daughter kept crying. "You don't get it Mom. No one likes me and I am the dumbest kid in the class." Her mother felt like crying herself but kept reassuring her daughter that it would get better. Monday afternoon Brenda came home angry again and claiming that she was never going back to that school again. The next morning she had a headache and a little fever, so her mother thought it was best if she stayed home. After all, the previous week of school had been hard for her. Maybe she was coming down with something.

The weeks went on, and every morning presented a challenge to get Brenda to go to school. She continued to dislike her teacher, do poorly in school, and be left out of social activities with her classmates. Her peers told her they felt like she was always disrupting playground games. She soon became the target for teasing by two of the classroom bullies. Her mother and father would tell her, "You need to get ahold of yourself. You can do better at school than you're doing." Her mother suggested that they go shopping for new clothes that were more like the other girls' clothes. Both parents told her, "You need to be nicer to your friends, then maybe they'll want to play with you."

Mom worried about Brenda, whereas Dad got back into his work and told Brenda, "You need to live with it." He didn't talk to her much about school anymore, but Mom waited anxiously every day for Brenda to get home. Her mother would quiz her over who she ate lunch with, played with, and whether any classmates were getting together after school and whether Brenda had been asked, too. Brenda's self-esteem was at an all-time low. She felt sad all the time and was afraid to go to school. Worse, she was afraid to come home because of the "third degree" questioning she received from her mother. She also felt sad because her dad didn't seem interested in her at all. Soon she felt angry all the time and really didn't care if her dad got mad at her when she misbehaved. It seemed that was the only way to get his attention. On the other hand, the attention she got from her mom was based more on the problems that Brenda reported were happening at school. She got attention from both parents, but for all the wrong reasons. Neither parent knew how to help her.

ℰ◌

Cognitive Reasons for Depression

First, many parents ask me what I mean by "cognitive." Simply stated, *cognition* is thinking, knowing, and perceiving. Thus, the act of cognition is the act of thinking and perceiving something in our lives in the context of what we know about it in terms of the our past, present, and future. What we know about it may be accurate or it might be distorted. These perceptions set us up to have certain thoughts, leading to specific feelings and behaviors.

Cognitive theory indicates that negative thinking is a major reason for the development of depression. Several psychologists such as Beck et al. (1979), Ellis (1962), and Burns (1980) have made major contributions to the field. Although many authors have described cognitive therapy in simple terms, it should be kept in mind that it is a complex therapy that uses both cognitive and behavioral interventions. The first part of this chapter will orient you to cognitive theory. Then we'll adapt some of these techniques to assist you in using them with your children. I will draw my explanations from Ellis, Beck, and Burns. They wrote how your feelings are within your control because you can control the thoughts that lead up to them. Thus, the way you think and perceive occurrences in your life might be able to prevent depression as well as change other feelings. In fact, techniques helping you to change your thinking to improve your mood have been so successful that they're now used for numerous conditions.

It is very exciting that children (depending on their developmental level) can use these cognitive techniques for the same purpose. Research has shown that children diagnosed with depression can very effectively use cognitive techniques as ways of identifying negative thought patterns (Dujovne 1992; Nelson 2003), enabling them to change their feelings and learn how to cope with their depression. Beck et al. (1979) saw cognitive therapy as an insight therapy that helped people recognize their negative thoughts and beliefs about certain situations in their lives and how these thoughts relate to their feelings and behaviors. So, if they can identify these thoughts and change them to more positive thoughts, then positive feelings would result.

Cognitive Triad

Beck et al. (1979) identify three things that explain depression. They are the *cognitive triad*, *schemas*, and *cognitive errors*. The cognitive triad is felt to be central to how the person (a child, in this case) looks at themselves, their environment, and their future. Let's look at how the depressed child looks at these three things.

- The child views his- or herself negatively and thus feels worthless, deprived, or inadequate. For example, this is the child who talks about no one liking them and never feeling they can do anything right. "Why go out for basketball? The coach will never play me. He likes the other boys better."

- They interpret their interaction with their world and their environment in a negative way. For instance, any positive compliment or effort that happens toward this child is misconstrued by the child as being insincere. "The only reason you want to see me for this stupid therapy is to get money from my dad."

- The child views the future as negative. For example, the child questions if they will be successful in the future or feels impending doom. "I think my dad is going to get shot every time he goes out on patrol."

This triad seems to be pretty prevalent in our youth today. Don't blame yourself. If you think about the threats in children's lives today, you might better understand why they might doubt themselves and their futures. That is why it is so important to begin to help your child use these cognitive techniques so that the present and the future can be faced in a more positive fashion. It will be your way of arming your children.

Schemas

Basically, this is when a person consistently reacts to similar stimuli in different situations. Thus, a child can experience a situation and respond to it cognitively in a negative way. Subsequently, after several months or years, a similar situation may arise and the child will respond the same way they did earlier. The schema is the way the child perceives a situation. In other words, it is a consistent way the child responds to a situation cognitively.

In children without depression or with mild depression, they may try to look at a situation objectively and think through what that situation truly means to them. In more depressed children, the child will respond in a more negative way, using very little if any objective criteria in the interpretation of the situation. Thus there is very little connection to what is truly happening and their negative thoughts about it. This kind of pattern leads to distorted thinking (Beck et al. 1979).

Cognitive Errors

Negative thoughts and maladaptive beliefs have been described as "errors in thinking" (Weiten 1997) and "cognitive distortions" (Burns 1990). As I go through the list of these distortions, I'll use examples of how these distortions occur in a child. You'll probably also see a lot of these distortions in yourself— most of us do. All of us make errors in the way we think. I hope that once you become aware of these negative patterns, I can begin teaching you how you might help your child's thinking so that they can learn to cope more effectively. Now let's look at these distortions as I have defined them for children.

Burns (1990) identified the following common distortions. These lead kids (and grownups) to inaccurate thoughts and negative feelings.

All-or-Nothing Thinking

When these children have something happen in their lives that is tainted, they become discouraged because accomplishments have to be perfect. So for example, your child may make a B on a math test. Instead of being glad for a good grade, they begin thinking that they might as well have failed the test. Never mind the four other As they've made on previous math tests or the fact that a B is a perfectly good grade. If your child thinks this way, you may discover a sense of perfectionism in yourself, as children often learn this mode of thinking from their parents. You may find yourself worrying about what will happen to your child if they make anything less than straight As, and your child believes they must perform perfectly in school and extracurricular activities. Then they will become very sad if they can't be perfect at whatever they do. They are likely to think, "If I am not perfect, then I am the exact opposite. I am imperfect."

Overgeneralization

This is when a child believes that if something happens in one situation, then all situations that are similar will lead to the same occurrence. So your child may believe that because they had trouble reciting a poem in front of the class one time, that they will always have trouble doing anything similar. Maybe they struck out at the plate during their turn at bat. Now they're convinced that every time they get up to bat, they will strike out. This type of negative thinking can lead your child to believe they can't succeed at certain things, causing them to avoid similar situations.

Mental Filter

This is when a child can only see the negative in a given situation. For example, let's consider the ten-year-old girl who sings a solo in front of her church congregation. Her voice is beautiful. She does not miss a note, but by mistake she sings the second stanza twice. After realizing this at the end her performance, she leaves in tears. Her mother is concerned because the girl cries for several days and talks about how embarrassed she is that she made the error. In actuality, there were probably people in the audience who didn't even realize she had sung a stanza twice, and even if they did, they were impressed at how a girl this age could sing so beautifully and in front of such a large crowd.

Discounting the Positive

This is a distortion that I see in parents more than their children. Generally speaking, it is when someone gives you a compliment and you minimize it. So say your child's teacher tells you what a good job you've done helping with the Halloween party. You have actually spent several days organizing this party, but when the teacher says this to you, your response is, "Oh, anyone can do this." The other thing I have noticed in my practice is that parents that do minimize the positive have a hard time giving positive feedback to their children. I guess that if you don't feel good about what you're doing, it's unlikely that you will have enough positive energy to help your child feel good about what they do.

Jumping to Conclusions

Undoubtedly, this is one of the most common types of distorted thinking I see both parents and their children display. First let's look at you and how this may get in your way. This is when you decide something about someone or some occurrences without any evidence to support your opinion. Let's say you are a new soccer mom, and you attend the game. Some of the other soccer moms who have known each other in the past are off in a group talking. They come over and introduce themselves and then go back to the conversation they'd been having, about who will bring the refreshments at future games. They don't automatically include you on the list, so you decide they must be snobs and don't want to involve you with the refreshment responsibilities. The fact is, they were working from last year's list and inadvertently overlooked you. You don't say anything and they don't either. You have decided without checking it out that they are leaving you out, and you have made a quick judgment that they must be snobs. In the future you find it very hard to go to the games because you're convinced that the other parents must not like you. This is a little overgeneralization mixed with jumping to conclusions, don't you think?

Your child, on the other hand, may go to the game and predict that there is no way they can do well. They worry, "What if the other kids make fun of me, or what if I don't block a shot?" Unfortunately, this sort of predicting may end up becoming true. It's like a self-fulfilling prophecy.

Magnification

Parents often give their child so much attention for the problem they might have that they forget to help the child see what is good about themselves. For example, what if your child lived with terrible pain because of their rheumatoid arthritis. The child begins taking new medications and gradually the laboratory tests indicate that the disease is better. You, however, dwell on your child's complaint of pain. Not much is said about the positive things your child is doing in their life, like making straight As and performing for the honor band. If you recall from earlier in the book, when you give attention for something negative like these complaints and never recognize the positive in your child's life, then your child learns that the way to get attention is through complaining or being ill.

Emotional Reasoning

I see this a lot in children who are somewhat depressed or anxious. They jump to conclusions strictly based on how they feel. For example, let's say your child feels anxious every time they see storm clouds come up in the sky. The child believes that those clouds mean that there is going to be a tornado. So when they get those feelings, they go to the basement until the sky is clear, regardless of whether there really is a tornado coming. Or children that feel lonely may conclude that they must not be liked by anyone, even if there is evidence to the contrary. In other words, the children in both of these cases are reacting to the emotions they are feeling rather than the facts. Watch out— parents are as vulnerable to this as their children. If I see a child who does a lot of emotional reasoning, I'll most likely find that at least one and maybe both of the parents do the same thing.

Should Statements

This is when parents are always telling their children what they should or ought to do. Parents that use a lot of "should" statements with their child often feel pretty miserable as parents. They are always angry and their child is always feeling guilty or mad. So when you say to your child over and over again that they "should" do better on their grades, you end up setting yourself up to feel a lot of anger if they don't do well. You'll also have a child who feels guilty because they believe they can't measure up to your shoulds. Burns also identifies "musts, oughts, and have-tos as similar offenders" (Burns 1990, 9).

Labeling

Labeling is just that. You label either yourself or others. I see both children and their parents do this a lot. If a parent models this, then you can bet it won't be long before their child will be doing the same thing. An example is the child who gets up and miscalculates an equation on the board in front of the class. He responds in front of the whole class, "I am so stupid." It's not long before a few members of the class will be calling him stupid. A mistake that I hear parents make often is labeling their child's teacher. I heard a mother say to her child, "I don't think there is anything wrong with you, I just thing you have a dumb teacher." You can probably guess how much respect that child would have for their teacher after that.

Personalization and Blame

Parents are notorious for this type of distorted thought. Far too often they blame themselves for anything negative that happens to their child. For example, if a child doesn't seem to be popular the parent will ask me, "What have I done wrong to cause my child to lose friends?" Children will also blame themselves when things don't go well in their family. It's not at all uncommon for a child to blame themselves when their parents get a divorce. "If I had only been good, they wouldn't have gotten divorced." Boy, these are big burdens for both parents and children to carry. What guilt to live with!

Distorted thoughts about a situation cause problems because they cause a feeling and your child reacts to the feeling. Ellis (1962) taught us that it's not the situation that makes us angry, sad, and anxious but how we *perceive* that situation. So when your child says that their teacher made them feel angry enough to throw a tantrum, it's highly unlikely. It was the way the child perceived the teacher in a certain situation and what they thought about that situation that brought on the anger. So it stands to reason that your child needs to begin to learn how to become aware of what they are thinking about a situation and how these thoughts and perceptions affect how they feel. It also seems like common sense that if we can teach our children how to be more accurate about their perception of the situations in their lives, we will be offering them an effective way to change their more negative feelings into more positive ones. If your child has more positive thoughts then they will generally feel better about themselves and their world.

So now let's summarize. You now have an understanding of some of the cognitive distortions that can bring on negative feelings. You can see that if either you or your child fall into these thinking patterns it might be harder for you to be happy. Before we investigate further into how to help your child with these, I want to have you look at other things that influence your child's feelings. Once we have reviewed them, then let's look at some positive-thinking techniques that you might try at home to combat all of these pitfalls.

It's also important to realize that there are times when your child perceives things very accurately and it's a normal response for them to be angry or depressed. There are also times when an illness, parent's divorce, a death, learning disabilities, or a lack of friends are good reasons for your child to be depressed. What you want cognitive techniques to do is to help your child find hope and strength in handling those situations. Because you are such a good parent, you recognize when your child is struggling in a truly stressful situation, but you also want to make sure that your child is equipped to handle that situation.

Listening to Your Child

Parents often come to me concerned that their child has shut down and there is no communication between their child and them. What are some of the ways that you might assure that you have communication between your child and you? Communication involves a give-and-take interaction. In other words, it involves listening and talking with your child. Notice that I use talk *with* and not talk *to*. Talking with your child involves both of you talking to each other, not a one-sided relationship in which you are always telling them what you think. Remember, talking with your child is not possible unless you listen to your child first.

Children, and especially lonely children, often feel like no one is listening to them. The most important thing you can do to promote a relationship in which your child will let you know what is bothering them is to listen to them. This is not always an easy thing, but you will notice that if you are successful at this, your child will come to you and let you know what is bothering them. The message you give to your child is that you understand them and you value what they have to say to you. If you don't do this, then your child is automatically going to think you don't care about what is happening to them. Your child will shut down and seek refuge in their room. Often they will seek out other people to talk to, and sometimes these people are not the best influence on your child.

What are some things that will help you listen and convey to your child that you care?

* Listen to your child when they want to talk, not when it's convenient for you.

* Find a quiet place where you will not be interrupted by things such as their siblings, phones, or television.

* Give your undivided attention. In other words, don't be thinking about a number of other things while your child is talking to you. Your child can tell if you are really listening.

* Don't judge your child while they are sharing something. For example, if they are telling you how the teacher placed them in time-out and it wasn't their fault, don't begin wondering what they did to deserve this while they are explaining.

* Don't interrupt your child while they are telling their story. Let them talk. If you want to say something so that your child knows you're listening, then do something like this. "Wow, this was a hard day for you. See if I understand exactly what you have told me so far." Then reiterate what you have heard and allow your child to clarify the things they have said.

* Watch that you don't equate what has happened to you with what has happened to your child. There are times when you might disclose something about your own childhood, but the problem is parents get carried away. Many end up talking about themselves, not listening to their child. At this point, your child really doesn't care about what has happened to you—they want you to care

about what has happened to them. Appropriate self-disclosure can serve two purposes. One, it lets your child know you have not led a perfect life, and two, it gives you credibility for understanding what they are going through. So pick and choose times to tell your child about yourself and make it short and sweet. But be careful that these times are not interrupting the times your child needs for you to listen.

Don't you think your child is more likely to feel support from you if you listen and don't bombard them with lots of questions and information? Now let's look at how you can help your child with their feelings.

Your Child's Feelings

Now I am going to change some ways you may teach your child about their own feelings. Often, kids who are sad or depressed feel pressured to identify their feelings to adults. Then they become resistant to efforts to help them identify their sad feelings. Many children and adolescents either can't admit they are sad or may truly not see it in themselves.

Start off when the child relates something to you that has happened in their life. Try to help them identify how they feel about this. For example, say something like, "I bet that really made you sad, mad, happy, frustrated, etc." Make sure you know how they feel and not how *you* would feel in the same situation. For example, if you are depressed, you may misread the situation your child is describing. So be careful that you don't invest a lot of anger into a situation that happened to your child because you're feeling protective or because you're remembering a similar situation in your own childhood (reacting to your own schemas).

Children often tell me that they hate telling their mom or dad about something because their parent then makes an issue of it. The kids just want to be heard. You can identify their feelings in a subtle way if they are resistant to talking about their feelings. Let them tell you about what has happened and just listen.

At times you may be having a general discussion with your child, not about a specific upsetting incident, and you can say something to help them begin to identify how you think they are feeling. You can say things like, "You seem so happy. Tell me about your day." Another way to stimulate them to think about their feelings is to say, "What is that frown about? Are you mad about something?"

Other People's Feelings

Children that have a difficult time verbalizing how they may feel probably have a hard time identifying how others feel. I suggest that first of all you look at yourself and their other parent to see if you tend to be secretive about how you feel. Are you stoic? Are you private? Do you feel like you always have to be "on stage" and act like nothing bothers you? Be careful. Your audience is your child, and kids study parents very carefully. They take their cues from their parents about how they are supposed to display feelings. If you are happy, sad, and angry at appropriate times, then you are likely to see your children reflect that. If, on the other hand, you are a screamer and anxious, you are likely to see your child reflect that as well. You are your child's greatest teacher.

Children need to learn how to accurately appraise how others feel. Teach them to first of all to look at the faces of others. What do their facial expressions and speech tell them? What is their posture like and how do they walk? Is their hygiene good, and do they dress neatly? All of these things go into evaluating feelings. Teach them to look at others' behaviors. Do they cry easily? Do they smile? Do they laugh? All of this goes into accurately perceiving another's feelings.

Parents can teach their children a lot if they disclose some of their own feelings. So if something makes you sad, in most cases, it is okay for you to let your children know this. For you to display a happy face and be sad inside truly gives your child a mixed message. I am not telling you that you need to go into great detail as to why you feel a certain way, but it's good to be reasonably authentic about your feelings in front of your kids. By doing so, you give them permission to express their feelings in a healthy and honest manner.

How This Can Help

Learning about reading other people's feelings leads up to helping your child discover their own feelings and how they connect to the child's thoughts. Children are no different from anyone else. When they are depressed, they are often unaware that they have these feelings. Instead they show irritability, fatigue, and other signs of depression but never connect these to their feelings of depression. At times they will go to great lengths to deny that they feel depressed. Sometimes this is because they are too proud to admit it, but most of the time they don't see the connection to what is happening in their lives and their thoughts about those things and the feelings they are experiencing. Your child learning about their own feelings may take a long time. So let's get started on things you can do to help this happen in your child.

The Connection

Here is a neat exercise to help your child begin to identify their own feelings. Get a notebook or pad of paper to write on. First have your child describe what a feeling is. After they've done that and you've written down what they've said, then have your child come up with a list of as many feelings as they can think of and write them down. It is not unusual for your child to list those feelings that they tend to experience frequently in their own life. After they make a list, have them mark the feelings they tend to have a lot. Then give them some time to think of at least one situation that they connect to each feeling. Have them tell you about that situation and why they think they have that feeling in that situation.

Now you can teach them that the situation is not what is causing those feelings but what they are saying to themselves about that situation. In the event you're not totally sold on this connection between your thoughts and feelings, consider these two scenarios. Let's say you are going to your doctor. You have a sore throat and swollen glands. Before you go to the doctor, you're thinking of all the bad things that these symptoms might mean. The words "lymphoma" and "leukemia" flash through your mind. You probably have very anxious feelings. On the other hand, another time you are going to the same doctor and you have the same symptoms. But this time you say to yourself, "I guess I caught strep throat from one of my students. I hope he gives me an antibiotic so I feel better." This time you feel hopeful, relieved that you will finally be getting something that will make you feel better. You're probably not feeling extremely anxious. So now you can see how thoughts can change the feeling you are having about the same situation.

Automatic thoughts. So now let's get back to helping your child make this same connection. Keep in mind that sometimes, depending on the age of the child and their developmental level, this might take a little longer. Children may have a picture flash in their minds during certain situations that they may want to tell you about, or they may have just one word flash in their mind. Other children may have a whole sentence or phrase flash in their minds. You will soon discover that in certain situations those distorted thoughts may automatically flash in their minds, as they do in yours. The cognitive therapists call these "automatic thoughts" (Beck et al. 1979). These thoughts can be compared to a knee jerk or reflex when the doctor taps your knee with a percussion hammer during a physical. They're often so automatic that the child may not even be aware of them—only the feelings resulting from them. Once they have learned to connect thoughts to feelings then it's time to explore finding supporting evidence for their thoughts.

Gathering evidence. In order for your child to learn to find evidence to support this thought, you will have to ask, " What evidence do you have that this is so?" If they don't know what evidence is, you can ask them why they think the thought is true. Once they begin to learn that they need to come up with evidence that either supports or refutes their thoughts, then they need to learn to do something with that evidence. I see it much like gathering scientific evidence, a process they begin learning about early during their grade-school years. In other words, the thoughts are like hypotheses, and they need evidence to support them. If the child can't produce the evidence to support the thought, then ask your child to refute the thought and come up with some other explanation for a particular situation. This might change the way they react to a situation, changing the way they feel about the situation, and possible future experiences of the same situation. Coming up with another explanation is harder for children and may be something they will have to do at a later age, however there are some children that can do it. If your child can't do it, then you need to model how you might come to the same possible reasons for a specific situation. Besides, it will be good practice for you to start doing it, so that eventually you can be a role model.

Let's say the evidence is accurate; what are you going to do to help your child? You can ask them what is the worst thing that could happen if this is true about this certain situation. They may struggle with this. If they happen to identify something that is fairly benign, then they are likely to proceed with a whole new confidence, which obviously is really good for their self-esteem. If, on the other hand, they come up with something really negative that might happen, then you ask "What if this happens? What will you do?" Another thing to say is, "What if that happens, will you be able to stand it?" In other words your child is learning to look at outcomes and how they could possibly respond to them. Talking this way is a good "dress rehearsal." I consider these questions and responses a good way of learning self-arguments. At times children have a hard time with this, so I ask them what they would say to a friend if their friend were in the same situation? They can usually give you a very practical answer. If they come up with a good one for their friend, you can point out that this is the same answer they can give to themselves. Depressed children have a hard time seeing themselves as their own best friend. Children with good self-esteem soon realize they need to rely on themselves to look at the evidence and to know how to cope if something does happen in certain situations. This should be our goal for all children.

Let's look at some examples of how thoughts can influence the mood.

Situation	Thoughts	Feelings	Self-Argument
Gymnastics competition; Robin falls during her back flip.	I always mess up. I will never make that back flip. I am not as good as my teammates.	Inferior; Frustrated; Sad	That's the world of gymnastic competition. Sometimes I'm going to fall. Everyone falls at times. I'll just practice for the next competition.

So let's look at the chart and see if you can identify which kind of distorted thoughts is operating here. If you have identified the distorted thought as overgeneralization, you're right. The word "always" is the hint. You will usually see this result in feelings of inferiority, frustration, hopelessness, sadness, and other signs of lower self-esteem. Now ask your child, "What would you tell your teammate who was down on herself?" Together you will come up with something. Make sure your child is contributing to the self-argument with your guidance. It's amazing how kids can come up with good self-arguments that actually make more sense than what some adults come up with.

Now let's look at some conversations that might take place between you and your child to see if you can identify the automatic negative thoughts, the distortions, the consistent ways your child might respond to similar situations (*schemas*), and the feelings that result in these situations. I also hope that these interactions will help you to know how to respond to you child in similar situations. Here is an example:

Parent: How was your day at school?

Child: I feel so stupid. I came in third in my class spelling bee.

Parent: So, how many students were in the spelling bee?

Child: Well, all of the fifth graders. I guess about eighty.

Parent: So what is the evidence that you're stupid?

Child: Well, I guess I'm not exactly stupid, but I would liked to have been first.

Parent: What's the worst thing that can happen to you for being third?

Child: I won't be able to go to the regional spelling contest.

Parent: Can you stand that you can't go to that contest?

Child: I guess so, Mom.

Parent: How do you know that you can stand it?

Child: I did last year when I didn't go, but I was sure hoping I could this year. I guess I can always try again next year.

So now let's look at this. First of all, this child was labeling themselves as stupid because they did not come in first in the fifth-grade spelling bee. They were also using some all-or-nothing thinking. In their mind, they were going to be either a winner or a loser. Never mind that they were third out of eighty. This is an accomplishment in itself, which should be stressed to this child. Parents need to stress to their children that doing their best is what's important. If they happen to win a contest or make the top grade, they will see that as an extra. This attitude is best for good self-esteem. The other thing to look for is when a depressed child fails at a task. They will often make a big leap, going from failing at something to believing they are a failure. In other words, "Since I failed my test, I must be a total failure." These are pretty big consequences your child is imposing on themselves. Gathering evidence for and against the belief that they are a failure will help refute this damaging thought.

And here's a reminder not to get into the same pattern of thought as your child. You might be saying, "If I have a child with poor self-esteem, then I must have failed at my parenting. Therefore I am a failure." No, you're not failing at parenting and for sure you are not a failure. Don't do this to yourself. Parents who are failing don't seek out solutions to help their children.

Here is another example:

Child: Dad, the kids in the my class said that if I didn't smoke with them they would all hate me.

Parent: Now wait a minute—are you telling me that all the kids in your class are smoking?

Child: Well, most of them.

Parent: How many are smoking?

Child: Well, I guess about four of them.

Parent: Are there just four kids in your class?

Child: Um, no.

Parent: How many kids are in your class?

Child: Twenty.

Parent: I thought you said that all the kids in your class are smoking.

Child: Well, there are a lot.

Parent: Sounds like only a fifth of your class is smoking. What do you think would happen if they decided to not like you?

Child: Then I wouldn't have any friends.

Parent: You mean that these four kids are your only friends?

Child: I think so.

Parent: Who are they, Matt?

Child: Jack, Jim, Tony, and Justin.

Parent: I thought you just had John and Lynn over last week.

Child: Yeah, I did.

Parent: Well they're in your grade, and they are your friends, aren't they?

Child: Yes.

Parent: Sounds like you have two friends who don't smoke. I'll bet even more are your friends, but you just haven't thought about who they are.

In this case, the parent is trying to help his child to see that there is lack of evidence for his belief that all the kids in his class are smoking. His father helps him see that there are actually only a small number of boys who are smoking. On top of that, the father helps his son see that he has friends outside this group. Helping him realize this will help the child decrease his fears and maybe focus on the more positive aspects of his friendships.

Here is an example that has name-calling in it.

Child: Mom, Tammy called me a dummy.

Parent: Does that make you a dummy?

Child: Well, she called me one.

Parent: Look Kathy, if someone calls you a chair does that make you a chair?

Child: No.

Parent: Well, just because they called you a dummy does it make you one?

Child: No. I guess I'm not a dummy.

Here it's important for the parent to use a concrete example so their child can see that just because someone calls them something doesn't mean that's what they are. This is a mental strategy for your child to start using next time some kid calls them a name. It will help them put the teasing into perspective.

Now let's look at when your daughter has told you that all the boys in her class are mean because Mike threw a snowball at her. I like the following way of responding to this.

Child: Mom, I hate all the boys in my class.

Parent: Why? What's the problem?

Child: Well, Mike threw a snowball at me today and hit me in my back.

Parent: I'm sorry that happened. But you know, Mike is not *all* the boys in your class.

Child: Yeah, but they're probably all the same.

Parent: Well Honey, let's say you have a cherry pie and you cut it into six pieces. There is one bad cherry in the whole pie, and you happen to get the piece that has the bad cherry in it. The first bite you take has that bad cherry. So you refuse to eat any more because you assume that the whole rest of the pie is bad, when really the rest of the pie would have been the best one you ever had.

Child: So you mean that only Mike is mean, and maybe the other boys are okay. Mike is like the bad cherry.

This approach to overgeneralization can be used for older children and adults, too. It could help us with some of the biases people have today.

Here's another example of how you could show your child how to collect the evidence so they can fight their automatic negative thoughts.

Child: I am so clumsy.

Parent: Why do you say that?

Child: Because I fell down during my last ice-skating competition.

Parent: Does that one fall make you clumsy?

Child: Hmm ... well, maybe not. I guess I'm not clumsy.

Parent: Tell my why you don't think so now.

Child: Well, I skate a lot of times and never fall down. I even got second place at the last competition.

Parent: That's right. When you said that you were clumsy I could see your automatic thought. Then you looked for evidence of why that isn't true and saw that maybe you were jumping to conclusions. That was a great way to test whether your thought was true.

These have been some examples to help you see how you can respond to your child when they are upset. It's important to look for the irrational thoughts that are fueling the upset. Then you can give them more positive ways to respond to these situations. Now let's look at other strategies to help your child with their sad feelings or poor self-esteem.

Bolstering Cognitive Strategies

Children who are sad can use these cognitive strategies with the help of their parents but often their self-esteem is such that other strategies need to be used to help bolster them. For example, it's not unusual for these children to feel like there is nothing good about themselves. These next sections will incorporate some new information in order that you might help your child have improved self-esteem, which will help alleviate their feelings of sadness.

Affirm the Positives

Most children with poor self-esteem have a hard time seeing what is good about themselves. They either haven't been told what people like about them, or they are so sad that they use their mental filter or they discount the positive. I suggest that you first identify those things about your child that you feel are positive. If a parent tells me that they have a hard time doing that, then I suggest taking several days or weeks to work on it. You may want to begin by describing your child and what it is that you like about them. This is not the time to think about what you don't like or what changes you want to make. Stick firmly to the positives. To get the momentum going you might try starting with something that you might be taking for granted about your child. This might get you going and will help you to continue looking for the positives. These can be things about your child's appearance, behavior, and accomplishments. Remember—you don't have to feel like you have to come up with this list in a short amount of time. Take your time, and you will find that you will discover more things than you ever thought you would. Obviously, this also will give you the opportunity to use positive feedback, telling your child all the positives you're finding so that they can begin to see positives about themselves through your eyes.

There are times when a certain thing can be interpreted either negatively or positively, depending on how you perceive it. In other words, you have mental filters, too. These filters will influence what light you see your child in. Watch for your own distortions and check them out with another adult who knows your child so you're able to take every opportunity to identify the positives in your child.

I also like to ask children to begin listing what they like about themselves. Sad children have a very hard time doing this in one sitting. You might give them a nudge and say something like, "You know, I really like your beautiful hair." Then encourage them to spend a week or two listing their own positive attributes. If you're doing your homework assignment at the same time, they will hear all the wonderful feedback you are giving them and begin to incorporate it into their list and self-concept. What a wonderful way to continue to work as a team!

Schedule Positive Events

The lack of pleasurable activities is characteristic of a depressed child's life. They may not have the energy to plan their own activities because of the fear of failure or the fear of rejection. They tend to become withdrawn. This kind of lifestyle, in which they are only in their home and not getting involved in outside activities becomes reinforcing. Why? Because it relieves them of any anxiety about getting out and doing these activities. It becomes a vicious circle.

It should become an important responsibility for both you and your child to decide what activities they are going to have on a daily basis. All too often sad kids come home from school and become regular couch potatoes. Their time is spent watching TV, playing electronic games, or playing on the computer. Little time, if any, time is spent on homework, outdoor activities, and extra-curricular activities. Soon these children have only themselves to relate to. Their social skills wither, they're bored, and they dwell on their negative thoughts.

When planning the activities for your child, make sure you schedule them so that they have to get up and out of the house at certain times. These activities should include sports, clubs, play with friends, and of course their homework. Once they rediscover how fun some of these activities can be, then you can make the fun things contingent upon getting their homework done.

Now I'm afraid I have to talk out of both sides of my mouth a bit. This scheduling is an attempt to help the depressed child start activities that will get them off the couch. Here is the fine line: don't go to the other extreme in which you have scheduled your child in so many activities that they end up not having time for themselves to relax and they end up putting their schoolwork on the back burner. Make sure your child is learning to make friendships outside the school and plays "sandlot games" in which they have to make their own rules and have to learn to work out their own disagreements. Children that are overcommitted can begin to suffer from stress and fatigue, and they don't get the sense of self-efficacy that making up their own games, negotiating with peers, and letting their imagination wander can give.

So one side of my mouth says get your child busy while the other side says let them be creative and get their rest. It is a delicate balance, and a good parent like you will take the time to help your child find that balance.

Helping Your Child with Self-Statements

Self-statements are things you tell yourself about yourself, whether negative or positive. Many times the child gets into situations in which they need to be reminded of how wonderful they are, but there is no one other than themselves to help them do that. This is where positive self-statements come in. I encourage children to write out, on an index card or in a secret place in their notebook, positive statements that will replace the negative thoughts that come up so easily. Having them written in a particular spot will allow your child to read them periodically so they are reminded how truly neat they are. If there is a fear of some other kid seeing this written down, then rehearse with your child what they can say to themself periodically throughout the day that will affirm what a neat kid they are. They will need about two or three statements they can say to themselves at prespecified times to remind them how cool they are. Statements such as "I have somebody that loves me," "I am a good artist," "I am a good friend," "I am a good basketball player," and "I have beautiful eyes," are examples of such positive statements. I tell them that saying these statements to themselves at mealtimes and bedtime would be similar to taking medicine at mealtimes and bedtime. I also tell them to say their statements to themselves any other time that they are feeling sad or lonely or having any other negative feelings. Practicing this self-talk has been shown to result in enhanced self-esteem and positive feelings (Dudley 1997).

Coping statements are also important for children to learn to say to themselves (Dudley 1997). Remember, I told you earlier that our (yours and my) goal is for the child to become their own best friend so that they can say positive things to themselves. Such statements are important immediately after accomplishments so they can positively reinforce the child. For example, after your child gets back a test that they earn a B on and they have truly done their best, they might say, "Well done. I did my best," to themselves. Remember, sometimes kids might be with a coach, teacher, or some other adult who is not quick to give feedback about the child's accomplishments. So you are going to arm your child to protect themselves and give themselves their own positive feedback. Some parents ask what would happen if the child just gives themselves feedback that is not always accurate. In my experience, kids usually are accurate and honest with themselves. Remember, this is a kid who has traditionally been hard on and negative with themselves. I'm hoping they can learn to say some really great things to themselves. Otherwise, they shouldn't give any feedback to themselves at all. Again, this type of reinforcement seems to improve self-esteem.

Other Techniques to Improve Self-Esteem

There are other things that you can do to improve self-esteem, most of which have been discussed throughout the last chapter and here. Let's reiterate the important points before going on to teaching your child how to manage teasing. They are

* Identify the positives about your child.

* Reinforce appropriate behavior immediately after its occurrence.

* Help your child identify the positives about themselves.

* Maintain consistent discipline based on behavioral principles.

* Follow through on warnings.

* Help your child identify coping statements for the difficult times they encounter.

* If your child is misbehaving, punish the behavior—not the child.

* Make time for your child.

* Listen to your child.

* Listen for what your child is really trying to say.

* Listen to your child's feelings.

* Help your child connect their feelings to their thoughts.

* Help your child see when their thoughts are irrational.

* Establish clear rules for your child.

* Involve your child in activities that they can be successful in.

* Don't overextend your child in too many extracurricular activities.

* Help your child with academic problems.

* Help your child develop social skills.

* Get help for your own problems.

Now that we have looked at some cognitive techniques that can improve your child's life, let's look at some of the other things that will help them to manage stress. I will address some aspects of social skills and then look at deep breathing, relaxation, and visualization.

Helping Your Child with Social Skills

Many times, children who have depression don't have the energy or the insight to make friendships. Their moods affect people around them to the extent that their peers don't reach out and make friends with them, either. If you think about some of the symptoms of depression (like poor eye contact, fatigue, and irritability), you can see why other kids don't connect with these children. Soon this can become a vicious circle. The fewer friends they have, the worse they feel about themselves. I've found that one of the most important things to help a depressed child is to begin to help them feel more confident in social settings. Hopefully, if they can begin to understand what it takes to make friends, they will begin to feel more positive about themselves. The more positive they feel, the more likely other children will be to include them in their activities. Unfortunately, children usually don't like what they see as a loser. Children without social skills are likely to be included in the loser group. So let's begin helping your child with some social skills.

This can't be a comprehensive social-skills course, but I will highlight the things I feel would help your child in the social arena. To start, remember that social skills are really taught at home. If the home environment has individuals that respect one another then chances are your child will grow to respect others. However, if people in the home environment do not respect others and rarely use manners, then you can be certain that your child will reflect these behaviors and attitudes. When a child is in my office for cussing, I usually ask the parents where the child has heard those words. If the parents tell me that it's someone at home, but it happens only "every once in a while," I tell them that's really all it takes—just every once in a while. Think about the reinforcement dynamic I discussed earlier. Your child will always reflect what they are seeing at home.

Also bear in mind that social skills with playmates need to be explained and then taught in the home. Have a friend's child over for a couple of hours to allow you to give your child feedback on their behavior. Remember, this can't be done if you're cooking, talking on the phone, or just doing your thing while your child plays with this friend. Make time so that you can monitor the kids' play. This can be done very discretely, but it needs to be done. During that time, give them both feedback during their play for sharing and any other positive behaviors you observe. If for some reason they get out of hand, be sure to give them time-outs. If your child thinks that they will never be given time-outs when a friend is over, then they will take advantage of those times and misbehave. After all, your child is only human. Also make sure that your child learns how to share, but also how to cooperate with friends during games. Lots of good feedback for these behaviors will result in lots of on-the-spot learning. Notice I said that the play date should last about two hours. I have a reason for that. If you have a friend over for too long, the kids may get tired of each other and the visit can end up on a bad note. If that happens, then it might be harder to get together next time. Keep it positive as much as you can.

Next, teach your child to respect other people's personal space. If your child is one that likes to put their hands on others, tell them to imagine that people have a bubble around them and that every time they put their hands on another person it will end up bursting the other person's bubble. Help them try to make every effort not to pop the bubble.

Eye contact is another important skill to teach a child. Children with low self-esteem and depression will many times have a hard time looking others in the eye, especially in a one-on-one situation. It's important to teach the child that if someone is talking to them, they need to look that person in the eye to show that the child is interested and participating. Really, the best way to convey this is to look at the other person. This does not mean staring at the person, but looking at them with some brief breaks in the eye contact. I like to teach the child how they might feel if someone was talking to them and they didn't act interested. I do this by having them begin telling me about their day and then I start looking around the room and not at the child. Then I ask them how they felt. The child also needs to be reminded that when the teacher is talking or the coach is coaching, watching them will show that the child is paying attention. This indication often results in more positive feedback and opportunities to learn and to play. This positive attention can really help improve the child's self-esteem. Finally, remember the essential key to this is that when your child is talking to you, act like you're interested, giving them your undivided attention. Again, they will learn from you.

Verbal social skills are not always emphasized in the home. Parents need to be aware that their child needs to learn to use the proper loudness and tone of voice in order to be accepted by others. If your child is always loud, then people aren't going to want to be around them because they are always drawing attention to themselves. If, on the other hand, your child is shy and can hardly be heard when talking, people will soon begin to ignore them. Children need to learn that the volume and tone of their voice is an essential ingredient in making friends and being respected by others.

I am also amazed at how children with low self-esteem rarely remember other people's names. It's not a secret that children who are more popular know people's names, young and old alike. Teach your child to greet and say good-bye to people using people's names. And don't forget the proper use of "excuse me" and to stress "please" and "thank you." While using these courtesies, they should remember to maintain eye contact and respect for personal space. It all goes together.

Finally, overall body language is important for kids to be aware of. We have talked about eye contact, and that it should be used with good posture (sitting and standing), firm handshakes, and a walk that conveys confidence, not aggression. There are times when kids walk with an attitude because they want to be rude or because they are mad. They may stick out their tongue at someone or whisper or laugh when they are around someone they don't like at the moment. These are not good ways to respond to their feelings and are hardly mannerly. They are not behaviors that will serve your child. So your lesson is to teach your child to talk about these feelings rather than act out.

I recognize this discussion hasn't covered all of the things we can teach a child about social skills. An exhaustive examination is really beyond the scope of this book, and besides, there are whole books written on that. But I've tried to include the essential things to teach your child as they work on their self-esteem.

It's Time To Relax

There are several ways to encourage relaxation, from certain learned exercises to doing things that you and your child enjoy.

Also remember that the proper amount of rest and exercise and getting adequate nutrition are important to both maintaining energy and being able to relax. In the next section, we'll be looking at some specific techniques to help your child relax. I recommend that you make tape recordings of the prompts for the relaxation techniques and for visualization so your child can use them anytime. Let's start with deep breathing.

Deep breathing. Deep breathing is a nice way to learn how to relax when you are in an otherwise stressful situation. Children with depression or with low self-esteem often get stressed when they have to get in front of a class, go to school, or just be around people in general. Whatever might stress your child, this is a great way to begin to relax them. If they tell you they don't believe in it, say that's fine—but you would still like for them to try it. The deep breathing will sell itself if it's done right. You can also let them know that a lot of their sports heroes use this technique before their games or their at bats.

Breathing deeply is the required component of all of the relaxation exercises, and the child can do it no matter where they are. Lots of people think that a deep breath means either taking in a deep breath and holding it and then blowing it out quickly or taking in a quick deep breath and blowing it out immediately. Neither is completely right. In the first case, holding your breath can be uncomfortable and blowing it out too quickly does not do much for relaxation. In the second case, you're just taking a fast deep breath that doesn't do much at all. If you breathe this way long enough, you could even risk hyperventilation.

What you want your child to do is to take a deep breath in through their nose over a five-second period. Have them pull the air down to their belly button, so that their belly swells. They can also picture pulling it all the way down to their toes. Use whatever image seems to help them breathe slowly and deeply. You are using your diaphragm when you breathe like this. Then have them blow the breath out through their mouth, making sure that their lips are somewhat pursed. Don't have your child purse their lips in public, as this may increase teasing. They need to exhale slowly, over about seven seconds. Have them picture that they are blowing on a candle—not blowing it out, but enough to make it flicker. Or they can imagine they're blowing on a soupspoon filled with hot soup. If they blow too hard, they'll blow the soup out of the spoon. They need to blow slow and gently. Tell them they are bringing in the good air and blowing out the bad air. They may even want to say this to themselves. Now tell them to feel how their arms are getting heavy as they blow out the bad air. They feel heavy and like a rag doll.

Deep breathing should be practiced before getting out of bed, at breakfast, at noon, at dinner, and at bedtime. Most important, it should always be done when your child feels stressed and during those times they're afraid they're going to be stressed. Try it yourself. It works! But it works better if practiced and used consistently throughout each day.

Progressive muscle relaxation. Many times when people are stressed they don't realize how much they tighten up. And just think, if adults are not cognizant of how tight their muscles are during stressful times, then you know kids may not be either. I am going to present some steps to take that will help relax your child's muscles, encouraging them to relax not only their body but also their mind. Children are good at this—in some cases better than adults. First, ask your child to lie down somewhere that is quiet and peaceful for them. It's nice to have the light dim, but if your child does not want that, it's okay. Also, start off with your child's eyes open so they don't think this is weird. After you initially teach them this exercise, then they should close their eyes in the future. If your child has difficulty learning this exercise from you, then find someone else to help them with it. There are lots of counselors, exercise physiologists, and so forth, who know these exercises and can help your child with them. It would be a dollar well spent if the message gets through. Here are the steps:

1. Start by telling your child, "I am going to teach you how to make your body relax like a rag doll or a cooked noodle."

2. Have your child rest their head on small pillow, not too fluffy or big. Your child should have their arms down by their sides.

3. First have your child take three nice deep breaths all the way down to their toes.

4. Now have the child make a very tight fist. Have them do it for about five seconds. You can say, "Pretend you have a ball in your hand, and you are squeezing it. Hold it for a moment. Now let it relax. Can you feel the difference

when your hand is very tight compared to when it is loose and relaxed?" Now have them repeat this action with the other hand.

5. Direct the child to pull their hand back to make an "L" with their forearm. The child should tighten their forearm. Say, "Make it very tight and then let it go limp. Feel how relaxed your hand and your forearm are."

6. Continue with, "Now bend your right arm at the elbow and tighten your biceps or your upper arm. Make it as tight as you can. Take your left hand and feel how tight your bicep feels. Good job. Now let it relax. Now feel how relaxed your whole arm feels. It should feel heavy and limp. That's what I mean by relaxation. Compare it to your left arm. Doesn't your left arm feel stiffer than your right arm?" Then have the child repeat the sequence for the left arm.

7. Now ask your child to compare the two arms and tell you which feels the most relaxed. If they're the same, great! If one seems stiffer than the other (which is usually the case), repeat steps four through six for the stiffer arm. If your child is able to determine that it is only part of one arm that feels stiff, then repeat the exercise for that specific part.

8. Have your child take some more deep breaths.

9. Now have your child close their eyes and lift their eyebrows up toward their forehead. Tell them that they need to furrow their brow. Have them think about how tight their forehead feels. They can hold it for a moment, then relax. Can they feel the difference?

10. Next have them shut their eyes and tighten them as much as they can. Have them hold it, then relax. Ask them if their eyelids feel heavy. If they want to keep their eyes shut with those heavy lids, that's okay, or they can open them up. It might be easier for you to demonstrate the exercise if they can see you do it the first time.

11. Now have them wrinkle their nose and then relax it.

12. Next, they should tighten their jaws as much as they can. Have them hold it, then relax the mouth so the lower part of it hangs slightly open.

13. This time, ask your child to open their mouth as wide as they can, hold it, and then relax their lower jaw so that it hangs slightly open.

14. Now ask them to fill their cheeks with air, hold it, then relax.

15. Next they should put their tongue behind their front teeth and push hard, holding it there for a moment. Then have them relax their tongue. You can say, "Now feel how relaxed your face is. Is there any part that does not feel relaxed?"

16. They should go back to their arms and scan them. Are they still relaxed? If not, repeat the appropriate steps.

17. Have them pause to take some deep breaths.

18. This time ask them to put their chin down onto their chest. Have them feel with their hand how tight the back of their neck is. Explain that this is a common place for people to center their stress. Some stress headaches will arise from here. Then have them put their head back into the neutral position.

19. Next have them pull their head back into the pillow like they are looking at the ceiling, and then back to the neutral position.

20. Now they should tilt their head toward their left shoulder so the left ear is touching or nearly touching their left shoulder. Now back to the neutral position. Have them repeat this for the right shoulder.

21. Next have them turn their head to the left and back to the neutral position and then turn to the right and back to the neutral position.

22. Now ask them to stick out their chest and then relax.

23. Have them hunch their shoulders forward, then relax.

24. Now they should tighten their stomach and relax.

25. Next, they should tighten their buns (gluteus) and relax.

26. Now they should close their eyes and survey their whole upper body to see what still feels tight. If there is some muscle group that still has tension, then repeat the exercise for that part.

27. Your child should now pause for a few deep breaths.

28. Next, ask them to squeeze their right thigh muscles to the knees, hold it, and relax.

29. Now they can pull their right toes back so that the calf muscles tighten. Don't hold it so long that their legs get cramps. Now relax.

30. Now have them point their right toes down to stretch out the front of the right leg.

31. Now they should curl their toes and tighten them. Again, don't hold this so long that they get foot cramps. Hold the position and relax.

32. Repeat these leg exercises for the left leg.

33. Now have your child compare both legs. Which is the most relaxed? Repeat the exercises for the muscles that are not yet relaxed. Ask them to survey their whole body and determine what part is uptight. You can go through each group of muscles, having them find any remaining tension. Tell them that they can do this kind of survey themselves any time.

34. Finally, have them imagine they are a limp rag doll with very heavy arms and legs. Finish up with a big stretch.

This sequence should be practiced at least once a day. You notice I said at least once—twice would be good. Good times are before they get out of bed in the morning and before bed. Beyond that, they can do it any other time they are feeling stressed. Later these exercises can be tailored to fit the muscle group that seems to bother your child more, but it's always good to complete the full exercise as frequently as possible. Don't nag your child about doing it. When they do this and recognize that it helps, they will be sold.

Visualization. Now that you have taught your child how to do deep breathing and progressive muscle relaxation, we need to move on to visualization. This technique uses your child's wonderful imagination for the purpose of visualizing themselves involved in an activity that they find very relaxing. I have had children who go to the beach, snorkel, fly in a plane, go to their bedroom, sit in front of the fireplace, ride their horse, and a ton of other scenes. It's important that the activity chosen is your child's idea and not yours. So ask your child where they'd like to go to relax. Give examples like I have. Children have a hard time going to a peaceful place that they have never been to before. Let them choose where they would like to go in their imagination.

Let's say your child picks the beach. I want to demonstrate how we might help them to use that for relaxation. Help your child incorporate all the senses. I want them to hear the ocean, feel the wind, smell the sea, feel the sand underfoot, and hear the seagulls. In other words, the scene needs to be visualized in detail. Depending on the child, younger children will take much longer to develop these scenes, but if they are motivated, they can practice it with you and develop it in as great detail as you would and, because of their lack of inhibition, may visualize something even more vividly. Again, practice will help your child with this. So let's look at how this technique might work.

First, find a nice, quiet place in your house or elsewhere where your child can relax and perform their visualization. Initially, you will need to walk them through it, but later they can do it themselves. If they refuse to do it or get frightened or anxious while they are doing it, have them take a deep breath and tell them to discontinue it. Never force your child to do progressive muscle relaxation or visualization if they don't want to.

Parent: So you want to go to the beach to relax. What a wonderful idea! Where is this beach going to be?

Child: I think I'll go to a white sand beach in Florida.

Parent: That sounds wonderful.

Child: I'm walking down the path to the beach.

Parent: Is it far?

Child: No, it's right near my beach house.

Parent: What do you see?

Child: I can see the ocean, the blue sky, and the sun. Sometimes I see a seagull soaring in the sky.

Parent: What do you have on your feet?

Child: I have thongs on.

Parent: What do you feel as you walk?

Child: I feel the warm sand between my toes and under my feet.

Parent: What else do you feel?

Child: I can feel the sun on the top of my head and on my shoulders.

Parent: Does it feel good?

Child: Uh huh.

Parent: Now what are you doing?

Child: I am putting my chair on the beach so I can sit in the sun.

Parent: What do you hear while you do this?

Child: I can hear the ocean waves. I also hear the seagulls. Oh yeah, I can sometimes hear a boat off in the distance.

Parent: Is there anything else you want to tell me about this wonderful place?

Child: Well, I'm lying in the sun, and I have my feet buried in the sand. The warm sand really feels good on my feet. The sun feels good on my body. Sometimes I hear someone walk by. They might be talking to someone. I think I can smell their sunscreen. It smells like coconut.

Parent: I am going to let you sun for a while, but first I would like for you to take some deep breaths and relax your muscles while you lie there. When you're ready to leave this spot imagine walking back from the beach. Keep listening, feeling, and smelling. It sounds like a wonderful place. Enjoy it.

So this is what visualization looks like. It is not at all uncommon for a child to become so relaxed that they actually fall asleep. Children may verbally indicate to you they want to quit or they may become restless. When it is time to end their visualization, warn them that it is almost time to stop. Make sure they have concluded their experience the way they want to. Then, while they are still reclining or in the position for their visualization, they should open their eyes. Once their eyes are open, have them give a big stretch and sit up. It is not at all uncommon for them to be so relaxed that they seem a little groggy. That's a good sign. Now you try it and see what you think. I think you will be pretty amazed at how wonderful it is to get away to your own relaxation spot.

Other recommendations. Proper nutrition is important for all of us. A well-balanced diet that includes carbohydrates (such as fruits, vegetables, wheat breads, wheat crackers, cereal, rice, and potatoes), proteins (like meat, cheese, milk, and eggs), and some fats is necessary for a healthy body. Children who are too heavy or too thin not only bear the brunt of other children's teasing, but they are also set up for some major health problems. If your child has a special diet and you're not sure they adhere to it, take a look at your cupboards. It's important to buy the foods that should be on your child's diet so they're not tempted by foods that aren't good for them. I don't buy the argument I often hear, "What about the other members of the family?" They can go out and get their food desires met at a restaurant or at school. What happens to one member of the family needs to become a family affair.

Exercise is also important for children to remain both emotionally and physically healthy. Again, if you aren't exercising, you give your child an excuse not to do it. A minimum of a half hour per day is recommended for everyone. It would be nice if your child had physical education all through their school experience, but that doesn't necessarily happen. Therefore, they're going to need some encouragement from you. It's always important for depressed children to get regular exercise on a daily basis. It's essential for relaxation and to improve the mood. And what's good for the depressed child is also good for the rest of the family. I always tell parents that walking encourages talking, helping you both to get exercise and improve your communication. Try it with your child—it works.

Summary

We've been looking at the use of cognitive interventions, based on the connection of thoughts to feelings, for your child with poor self-esteem and depression. When these interventions are used with deep breathing, progressive muscle relaxation, and visualization, you'll have a strong defense for your child while they fight their low self-esteem and sadness. Although we're talking about these exercises for the sad child, they can also be wonderfully helpful for all children. Cognitive techniques have been proven to increase self-esteem, and there are now several emotional and physical disorders that cognitive therapy has been demonstrated to be successful in improving. Not only have these techniques been important tools for children, they can be enormously powerful for adults, too.

In the next chapter you'll become familiar with other possible diagnoses that may be appropriate for your child. Your doctor should consider these alternatives when the diagnosis of depression alone doesn't seem to fit. When you understand these other diagnoses, you will be better able to advocate for your child if they don't seem to be getting better and alternative explanations are being sought.

Chapter 7

When the Diagnosis Doesn't Fit

ᔐ *Tony's Story*

Tony had been seeing the psychiatrist who had diagnosed him with major depression for a few months. The doctor had placed the eleven-year-old on seventy-five milligrams of Zoloft. But in spite of the best efforts of Tony's psychiatrist and parents, numerous calls from his school were still coming in. One day Tony's teacher called to say Tony was in the office for fighting with another student on the playground. Three days before this, the teacher had called and said Tony had refused to do his schoolwork. The teacher was asking for help and requested that the parents come in for a meeting with her, the counselor, and the principal. Tony's teacher had not seen much change in Tony in spite of the medication. She never knew what mood Tony was going to be in when he got to school. One thing was for sure, she could tell the moment Tony walked in the room whether this was going to be a good day or bad day for her and for her class. She asked Tony's parents whether he was getting enough rest at night. She hoped the solution would be as simple as getting more sleep or eating a good breakfast. The parents were looking for reasons at school that could result in their son's problematic behavior. But at the end of the meeting, it seemed everyone was stumped. They agreed that maybe the thing to do was to go back to the psychiatrist and talk to him about the lack of progress.

As Tony's doctor heard the stories, he became concerned that maybe the right diagnosis hadn't been made or that Tony might have something else going on at the same time as depression. The doctor suggested that first they take Tony to a psychologist to determine what they thought. He also felt that Tony and his parents would benefit from therapy. The appointment was made and the evaluation started.

∞

The Next Step to Help

When parents begin to realize their child is not getting better, I find that they have a tendency to not do anything and think the problem will go away; or to believe that it is always someone else's problem; or to begin doing something, but not in a methodical way. It all comes down to many parents denying that their child has a problem as serious as everyone else thinks. On the other hand, some parents may panic and begin changing doctors and looking for a magic cure. My advice to you is to stick with a doctor who already knows your child and knows what has and has not worked while at the same time asking that doctor for some other ideas about what might help your child. In this way you can advocate for your child without changing so many elements that you can't tell what's working and what's not.

I have already discussed some cognitive and behavioral interventions that can be used with your child. Don't stop these. No matter what the diagnosis is, these are good, positive ways to help your child feel better and can do nothing but good. Remember that it's important for you to be sure to let your doctor know what interventions you're doing at home. More than likely your doctor will want to build their treatment plan onto these.

Once you and your doctor have discussed your child's diagnosis and what is being done for now, then it is important to discuss what other diagnoses might be considered that would look like depression but may not be depression. Also, there certainly is the chance that your child might have more than one diagnosis. For example, your child might have depression with anxiety or some other combination of different diagnoses with depression. This means there may be a need for your doctor to change the medication your child is taking and there may be a need for more intense therapy. Remember, chances are your child will do better if they have a combination of medication and therapy. Having knowledge about your child's diagnosis, medicine, and treatment will help you ask your doctor the right questions. This is important when seeking out answers to your questions and the school's questions. Chances are your child has a few questions about what is going on, too. Often they can't understand what is happening and are frightened about what is in store for them. Make sure the opportunity to ask questions is available for your child, too.

A Word for the Wise

All too often parents and doctors begin looking for even more clinical diagnoses when a child just doesn't seem to be getting better. Be sure that the obvious things about the child's life are looked at first before looking at more serious diagnoses. For instance, make sure your child has had a thorough physical that includes consideration of any medications the child may be taking. Make sure you are in communication with teachers, counselors, and the school nurse when determining if anything is going on at school that might result in your child being unable to cope with events in their life. For example, watch for your child being left out of peer activities, struggling with academic subjects, or being the brunt of teasing. Many parents are so busy that some of the more obvious social and school information escapes them. Instead of having major behavioral problems or mental-health problems, your child may just be desperately trying to cope with some intolerable things at school or at home. Look for the obvious first, then if all of that seems normal, take the next step and look for other clinical diagnoses. In any event, an unbiased professional's services may be needed to help you and your child get to the truth.

The Other Diagnoses

In order for me to help you see what some of these other diagnoses will look like, I am going to use a case example for each one. These descriptions should help you think about what else might be bothering your child so that you can report your suspicions to your doctor. You may discover even more than one mental-health problem that might resemble your child's problem. Your child may have one, two, or more diagnoses. Up to this point, the case examples have hopefully illustrated what a child looks like with either depression or low self-esteem. Now let's start looking at case examples of other emotional problems children are afflicted with.

Attention Deficit Hyperactivity Disorder (ADHD)

ℰↄ *John's Story*

John is a nine-year-old boy who has always been extremely active. If he isn't running around the house, he's jumping from the furniture. Since he was four years old he has required stitches in his forehead once and a cast on his left arm. Both of them came about when he was jumping off of something. Teachers, coaches, and Cub Scout leaders all complained that John was always blurting out answers, not awaiting his turn, and interrupting others when they were talking. Coaches were especially frustrated because John had a hard time following through with the instructions for very simple plays for his basketball team. It seemed he was always at the wrong place at the wrong time. Teachers complained that John was having a hard time following the verbal instructions for his schoolwork. Assignments were not being completed according to the instructions—or not being completed at all. At times John would get an assignment done at home but for some reason he would misplace it or lose it between home and school. His parents also complained about John not following through with their requests. "It's like he starts out to do what we ask and then gets sidetracked."

Teachers commented that it seemed like John was doing a lot of daydreaming in class. They noticed that when they were teaching, John would be in "his own little world." Often he would be tapping his pencil or just sitting and chewing his nails. During quiet time in class, John seemed to hear any little noise that was made. He was so easily distracted. If he wasn't making some comment about the noise, he was often up and wandering around while the other students were completing their studies. He would do things in class to entertain the other students, irritating his teachers by disrupting the class.

John's grades were average, but his teacher felt that he could be an A or B student if he'd just do his homework. His parents were frustrated trying to get John to do that homework. Most of the homework was actually schoolwork that John should have gotten done at school. Because of his talking and distractibility, he ended up taking work home in addition to his required homework. His parents believed he should be able to get all this homework done in an hour but because of his dawdling, it usually took him about three hours. There was a lot of fighting about homework. His parents reported that unless one of them was there at all times, John wouldn't complete his assignments. It seemed to his parents that John just couldn't organize his time to complete the assignments. Not only did he have trouble organizing his time, but his teacher often complained that his desk was always a mess. His parents could well imagine, because they complained about the same thing related to his room.

$$\mathcal{SO}$$

Criteria for Diagnosis

The *DSM-IV-TR* (2000) and other research (Barkley 1996; Whalen and Henker 1998) have determined a number of criteria by which a diagnosis of ADHD can be reached.

* **Hyperactivity.** This means the child is always on the go, jumping, fidgeting, running (at inappropriate times), exhibiting restlessness, and talking constantly. Also, the child is out of their seat and bothering others when they should be sitting quietly.

* **Short attention span.** The child can't sustain attention long enough to follow through with requests at home and at school. This results in their not completing school assignments and failing to complete home chores. They can't focus on things in a classroom because of their consistent tendency to focus on extraneous stimuli. Additionally, they lose things such as books, completed assignments, and personal belongings.

* **Impulsivity.** This is demonstrated when the child does not wait their turn. They often interrupt others, blurt out answers, and disrupt others. Adults in the environment have concerns about their possible dangerous behavior. Frequently, the child's behavior is geared toward getting attention using clowning or aggressive behavior. If they get in trouble, they may refuse to admit responsibility for their actions.

* **Other.** These children often have problems with self-esteem. Their life consists of getting a lot of attention for negative behavior. Like the child with depression, they also have poor social skills.

Exceptions to the Rule

Attention deficit doesn't always have to have daydreaming, impulsivity, and hyperactivity. It can come in a lot of different forms. It can be manifested in hyperactivity and impulsivity as the major problems, or you might see it as your child is simply unable to focus. Because it comes in so many different forms it's easy to miss.

Bipolar Disorder

ஸ *Tiffany's Story*

Tiffany is a twelve-year-old girl who was originally diagnosed with attention deficit hyperactivity disorder. Her parents and teachers saw her as quite inhibited. She would do and say things that seemed so impulsive. Teachers reminded her often that bragging was not good manners, but those reminders didn't seem to make any difference. Tiffany would just do it more. Often when she was reprimanded, she would become quite argumentative. Her parents reported she was hard to discipline because she would pout and scream at them in response. They found themselves taking the path of least resistance, letting her get away with things. Recently she was drawing on her arms and ankles. Other times she would take a straight pin and carve her initials and her boyfriend's initials into her skin. Her parents reported they could not get enough rest because Tiffany would stay up until one or two in the morning and be back up between five and seven that same morning. She never seemed to get fatigued. When her parents asked her to try to get more sleep she would respond by screaming and calling them names.

Finally, her parents decided it was time to discipline her, so they agreed that they would tell her she would have to be in bed by eleven. She refused to be compliant and continued with the late hours. A few days after they'd made this request they received a phone call from the school attendance office. The attendance secretary told Tiffany's parents she had not been at school for three days. The secretary said she had received a phone call from someone claiming to be Tiffany's mother and saying that Tiffany had mononucleosis and that it would be a few days before she would return to school. Her mother and father told the school they had not made the call. The next day they decided to come home from work at lunch to see what their daughter was up to. She would leave like she was going to catch the bus for school, but she was back home when they got there. They confronted her and Tiffany told them that she had only missed school that day. When they found her she was putting on some heavy makeup that included very dark eye makeup and bright red lipstick. They were also appalled at the outfit she had on. In addition to her very tight blue jeans, she had on a crop top that showed her pierced belly button. They hadn't known she had pierced anything but her ears.

When they took her for professional help the psychologist asked if these were new behaviors for their daughter. As Tiffany's parents reflected, they realized their daughter had long experienced extreme mood changes, sometimes changing as frequently as several times in one day. They rarely had a clue for the cause of her mood—it just changed. They also noted that if she wasn't acting out that way, she seemed depressed. Her mother told the doctor that she had a sister who had been diagnosed with manic-depression (now referred to as bipolar disorder) when they were growing up. Tiffany was a lot like her. That sister had committed suicide when she was twenty-one. Tiffany's mother's greatest fear was that Tiffany was becoming just like her aunt. She wondered if maybe Tiffany's diagnosis was not right, or if she had something in addition to her diagnosis of ADHD.

℘

Criteria for Diagnosis

As you recall, I talked about bipolar disorder in chapter 1 as a type of mood disorder. You might want to look at that description as it relates to a continuum of depression. Now I want to describe it in more detail.

You may hear from friends and even from some professionals that bipolar disorder is not seen in children. That may be their opinion, but presently there are books and articles clearly describing this as a possible childhood disorder. Additionally, there are several centers in the United States that have bipolar disorder in childhood as their research focus. So let's look at what they are reporting as characteristic of this disorder in childhood.

Early symptoms. As you may remember, bipolar disorder is characterized by the swing between depressed mood and manic mood (including hyperactivity, extreme loquaciousness, and grandiosity). Well, often the child with bipolar disorder may look like they have simple depression in the early stages of their disease because you're not aware of the manic swing. However, when your therapist takes the psychological history of your child, it may become evident that one or more manic episodes have been present prior to the depression but have been misinterpreted as acting out, rage attacks, or other behavioral problems. The mood extremes may shift so rapidly from the depression to the manic states that it can be hard to tell what is going on with your child. When mood changes this quickly your therapist may refer to your child as being in a *mixed state*. In other words, the depression and the mania are occurring at the same time (Papolos and Papolos 1999). The rapidity with which these extreme moods change in the child is described as a major sign of bipolar disorder of childhood. This rapid change in mood states is generally not seen in adults and is much more common in children. Thus, if you're expecting that your child will act like adults you know with bipolar disorder, you may miss the symptoms your child is displaying.

Unique childhood symptoms. Nighttime becomes a major concern for these children. They are fearful of having nightmares. They may sleepwalk, exhibit night terrors, or be particularly restless during their sleep. One mother described her child as getting up in the middle of the night and turning all the lights on in the house and returning to bed. The child was unaware that he'd done this when he woke up the next morning. Another child was found getting up in a dreamlike state in which she collected all the knives from the kitchen drawer and hid them under her bed. Although she said she didn't remember doing this, she did say that she frequently had nightmares in which a gang broke into her family's house.

Papolos and Papolos (1999) described the content of the dreams of these children as having a lot of fights in them and having vividly bloody scenes. The child's heightened anxiety seems to make the scenes from these dreams imprint like indelible ink. Children carry these scenes from their dreams to their awakened state and talk about them in great detail. Many times parents and teachers become quite fearful about what the child is talking about and other times they feel the child is making up an elaborate tale about their dreams just to get attention.

Soon daytime is filled with the child talking about the death of others and a fear of their own death. Other times, parents describe their child as suddenly having a rage attack when the child seems to not get their way over something fairly minor. These rages may last several hours and include kicking, hitting, biting, breaking furniture, and destroying others' personal belongings or their own personal belongings. Parents have told me about having to take the door off of their child's room because of the child's tendency to lock it and subsequently break windows and kick or hit holes in the wall. These parents will talk about how they are scared about what the child will do to themselves during these attacks. Other parents talk about rage attacks just coming out of the clear blue. They try to think back and determine what may have provoked the attack, but they just can't come up with a reason. All of the parents talk about how the child looks out of it during the attacks. They are glassy eyed, and at times the parents question if their child is having a seizure of some type. This may be questioned by your doctor too, since many times these children will be quite fatigued after one of these attacks and may take a long nap afterwards. Additionally, the child may experience a headache along with the fatigue. Because of these symptoms, your child may be referred to a neurologist to rule out a seizure disorder.

Symptom sequence. Although it seems like these children are not seen until they are nearly teens or are teens, parents will tell me that their child has always been different. Many times they can go back in history and describe their child as an irritable infant or a toddler that often threw temper tantrums. The child's mood has always been labile. Often, as parents, you begin questioning your own parenting abilities and search for what things you have done wrong that may have caused such an unhappy child. Remember, this is not a time to question yourself. It's not likely that you have done anything that has caused this. You are doing what is needed—you are attempting to get the right diagnosis for your child's problem. This way the right therapy can be started to help support you in your parenting.

Suicidal ideation. It's not at all uncommon to hear children with this disorder talk about being better off dead, and it happens at all ages. Talk of suicide should always be taken very seriously. As I have said earlier in this book, when a child talks about wanting to commit suicide, *watch them.* Children with bipolar disorder in a mixed state (agitation and depression at the same time) not only have the depression to lead to a suicide attempt but also are experiencing the agitation and increased energy that could enable them to complete it. If you think your child is talking about death more, tell your doctor. Get help to decide just what needs to be done. If you have a child talk about suicide suddenly, take them to the nearest emergency room to have them evaluated, and don't take your eyes off of them. Desperate children act fast and impulsively.

Suicide warning signs. Here are some things to watch for in your child that mean they may be at risk for suicide.

- Talks about being better off dead
- Appears depressed
- Talks about wanting to kill themselves
- Talks about death
- Becomes isolated
- Cries more
- Hygiene becomes poor
- Appetite changes (increased or decreased)
- Sleep habits change (increased or decreased)
- Shows more rage and irritability
- Grades decline
- Is lonely and has no friends
- Is bullied at school
- Uses alcohol or drugs
- Gives away personal possessions
- Writes about very sad things in school
- Writes notes about wanting to die
- Makes artwork that has very sad content
- Death in the family or of a best friend
- Classmate commits suicide
- Idol commits suicide
- Previous suicide gestures, such as cutting their wrists
- Previous suicide attempts

* Parents get a divorce

* Has a special-needs sibling who requires a lot of the parents' attention

* History of being abused

* History of a parent being abused

* History of a parent with drug or alcohol addiction

* Family history of suicide attempts

* Has no future plans

* Firearms in the home

Remember, if any of these warning signs or a combination of these signs occurs in your child's life, seek professional help *immediately*. Let your professional decide your next step. Also, take all firearms out of the home. It is not good enough to just lock them up. Any child can find your hiding place and can figure out how to pick your "childproof" lock. In addition, get rid of all potential poisons, medications, and knives to make your child safe.

In chapter 4, I presented a suicide-prevention contract. It's very important that you make this contract with your child if your child is depressed or has any of the warning signs of suicide. In addition, it's crucial to take the child to see their doctor as soon as you see any of the warning signs of suicide. If you feel they are in imminent danger of hurting themselves then take them to the nearest emergency room so they will be safe. Sometimes parents ask, "What if they won't go? They're too big for me to force them." In these cases, the parents should call the police or an ambulance and let the professionals handle it for them. Remember, it is always an emergency to get help for your child when they're not sure they want to live anymore. If you're not sure if it's an emergency, then let the doctor or the therapist decide. Remember to ask yourself, "What is the worst thing that could happen if I don't act on my child's scream for help?" Your answer should be obvious.

If this still does not fit the description of what you're seeing in your child, then let's look at some other psychological diagnoses that alone or in combination with the other diagnoses may seem more like your child.

Oppositional Defiant Disorder (ODD)

ஒ *Jessie's Story*

Jessie sat in my office with his arms folded and stared at me. His mother told me that he didn't want to be there but had told her he would come just this once. If he came to see me, he wanted his mother to just leave him alone. His mother described Jessie as having problems both at school and at home. He was in the fifth grade and the teachers had concerns because he refused to do his classroom assignments. When asked to do something he would simply say no and cross his arms. He spent more time in the principal's office than he did in the classroom because of the constant disruption he caused. This had been typical behavior for this ten-year-old boy. At first he was sent home each time he caused a ruckus. Jessie soon learned this was a pretty good way to get out of school. Once the principal learned that he was just going home and watching TV, they decided that there was probably a better approach to this problem. Now Jessie had to sit in the office without a lot of contact with people. He ate his lunch there. He lost his recess privileges and at the time of his visit to me, he had lost his privilege to go on a school field trip. His parents thought this was outrageous and decided that they needed some outside help. Jessie thought that if he went once to a therapist that maybe he could get all of his privileges back.

His parents described Jessie as always being negative about everything going on in his life. Jessie had a history of cussing his mother out. Anytime she would ask him to do chores, he defied her and left the house. Jessie's mother called his father and asked him to come home in order to regain control of Jessie. Sometimes this worked and other times it would result in Jessie having a major temper tantrum.

Other times when Jessie was less belligerent, he teased his siblings continuously. He tripped his younger brother when he was simply walking by Jessie. When Jessie was reprimanded for teasing his brother, he would say that his brother had bothered him first. Other times Jessie would demand to have the channel changer when his sister was watching television, and when she didn't give it to him, he would twist her arm until she gave it to him. If that didn't work, he would go to her room and knock everything off her shelves.

The first time I saw Jessie I noted that if he was asked a question, he would respond by repeating the question. He refused to answer any questions during his first visit but finally agreed to play a game of checkers. During subsequent visits, his parents came without Jessie so that I could begin working with them on some parenting strategies. The goal was to make them very consistent in their discipline and I also helped them provide similar discipline. Most of all, I wanted to help the mother become as good as the father at disciplining so that Jessie didn't see himself as having so much power over her. Additionally, we made plans to include the school in a discipline strategy for Jessie. After a few visits where I could observe Jessie closely, I told the family that I was certain that Jessie had oppositional defiant disorder, also known as ODD. In other words, he was a strong-willed kid and noncompliant to requests made of him. Many times this diagnosis exists at the same time with depression or bipolar disorder.

80

Criteria for Diagnosis

The *Diagnostic and Statistical Manual of Mental Disorders IV* (*DSM-IV-TR* 2000) lays out the criteria for the diagnosis of ODD. These criteria are supposed to have been present for at least six months prior to the diagnosis. Take note when a child displays the following:

1. Open defiance to requests made by authority figures

2. Negativistic behavior

3. Numerous temper tantrums

4. Resentment about having to do things that are asked of them

5. Argumentative responses towards authority figures

6. A tendency to blame others for their own mistakes or when they get reprimanded

7. Is annoying to others and seems to be annoyed by others

8. Exhibits spiteful and vindictive behavior

As you can see, Jessie exhibited several of the criteria. Your therapist must identify at least four of the aforementioned criteria before they can consider the diagnosis of ODD.

Anxiety Disorders

❧ *Julie's Story*

Julie sat in her room on a Sunday evening crying because her stomach was starting to hurt again. Her mother could not understand this because Julie seemed fine all weekend and now, on Sunday night, she was suddenly complaining that she didn't feel good. These sudden ailments seemed to be happening more and more often. Her parents were perplexed as to why Julie felt good during the weekend and then became ill on either Sunday evening or Monday morning. They really didn't feel she was making it up because, after all, she complained of dizziness, nausea, and stomachaches and sometimes actually vomited. Julie was taken to the family doctor on numerous occasions, but she seemed as perplexed as Julie's parents. The doctor referred them to the local pediatric gastroenterologist, who performed an endoscopy. The report was normal. He prescribed antacids and encouraged Julie to go to school, but Julie's parents found it increasingly difficult to get her to go. She cried, screamed, and on more than one occasion locked herself in the bathroom. It was just easier to let her stay home from school. It got to the point where she was missing two to four days of school each week.

Her mother recalled that when Julie was six years old she had a hard time separating from her mother. She slept with her parents every night. If her mother and father wanted to go out for the evening, she would cry until she made herself sick enough to vomit. It became easier for her parents to stay at home than to go out. Soon their marriage became strained because they rarely had time for themselves or each other. Each parent took their own night out alone or with friends. Their family doctor suggested that they find a babysitter that Julie could get used to. After about one month Julie would allow her parents to leave, but she still cried for an hour after her parents left. On the other hand, her parents tended to worry about Julie the whole time they were gone and would call frequently while they were out.

Not only was Julie's father worried about his daughter, but he worried about his wife's behavior as well. If a storm was forecast while she was out, Julie's mother would call frequently to make sure the babysitter was listening to the weather channel. Many times Julie's mother would take Julie to sleep in the basement for fear something would happen in the middle of the night and they would not wake up. Julie's father decided that rather than arguing with his wife about her overprotectiveness, he would just let it go. It seemed the best approach for keeping peace in the family.

The doctor heard the history of Julie's fears and her mother's fears and decided to refer each one to a psychologist for an evaluation. It was not long afterward that they both received cognitive behavioral therapy and were started on antianxiety medications. After a few months they both showed significant improvement.

ℰℑ

Criteria for Diagnosis

There are numerous types of anxiety disorders, but we're going to focus on generalized anxiety disorder, which includes overanxious disorder of childhood (*DSM-IV-TR* 2000). This specific diagnosis is presented here because of the common co-occurrence it has with the diagnosis of depression in children. As I have said earlier, it is rare that a child (or an adult for that matter) is diagnosed with one specific mental disorder. There is usually more than one thing going on. Now let's look at what you might see in the child who suffers from anxiety. In order for these to be considered as diagnostic criteria, they must have occurred for at least six months. Let's consider the following from the *DSM-IV-TR* (2000) and Jungsma et al (2000).

1. The child seems preoccupied with worrying about things (like storms or burglars) and events (like school).

2. They talk about being sick (having nausea, vomiting, diarrhea, being dizzy, and so forth).

3. The child reports that they can feel their heartbeat, shortness of breath, and dizziness. A psychologist may refer to this as being "hypervigilant." In other words, the child is aware of bodily changes that the nonanxious child would never be aware of.

4. The child seems hyperactive and quite restless. Teachers report that the child does not pay attention in school and wonder if the child might have attention deficit problems.

5. The fears of the child interfere with their daily living and daily activities because the child is refusing to leave their home.

6. They have a hard time separating from their parents and worry about being abandoned.

7. The child has trouble falling asleep and staying asleep. They frequently talk about being worried about sounds they hear or the shapes they see in the dark.

Other common problems found in the families of children experiencing this type of anxiety will include the following:

* One or both parents suffer from anxiety, too.

* There is a family history of marital problems.

* One or both parents express an excessive amount of guilt regarding occurrences in their family or other negative happenings in their life.

* Your child may suffer from a functional medical diagnosis. This means that the physical symptoms the child feels are real but an organic cause can't be found. The symptoms seem to increase with stress and worry. Irritable bowel syndrome or functional dyspepsia are examples of these types of diagnoses.

There are other anxiety disorders that are seen in childhood. Such things as obsessive-compulsive disorder, panic disorder, and agoraphobia can be seen in children. Your child may exhibit symptoms that look like these disorders, but doesn't necessarily have the disorders. So, it is essential when your child is being evaluated for symptoms of anxiety that information about such things as a medical illness, medications, or substance abuse be ruled out. These things can lead to anxiety symptoms which may be confused with an actual disorder. Remember to share all of this type of information with doctors, nurse practitioners, and mental-health professionals so that an accurate diagnosis can be made. Only what is shared can be taken into consideration when a diagnosis is being made.

Post-Traumatic Stress Disorder (PTSD)

ℰ **Mandy's Story**

Mandy was a seventeen-year-old who was driving and following her best friend to school on an interstate highway. It was extremely cold out and had been snowing throughout the night. She saw her friend Becky pass a truck and suddenly begin to slide into the truck. Then she saw her swerve away from the truck; Becky's car flipped three times in the air and landed on its side. Mandy slowed down but saw the truck and several other people stop and run to her friend's car. Mandy stopped and ran to the car as several men tried desperately to get Becky out of the car. People were yelling, "Get an ambulance." Mandy stood by the accident as if she were frozen. She watched as they pulled Becky from the wreck while supporting her neck. Mandy didn't see her move but heard one of the rescuers say, "She's still alive." Becky didn't move. Mandy walked away from the accident as she heard sirens in the distance. She got in her car and went to school where she told others about the accident. In a matter of fact way Mandy told them that it was Becky.

She walked off and went to her first class, where she sat as if in a daze. Her teacher asked her if she was okay and she said yes, but the teacher heard what Mandy had just experienced. She recognized that Mandy seemed out of it and took her to the school nurse. Mandy's mother was called and she came and took Mandy home. Mandy's mother worried because Mandy didn't want to talk about the wreck. She wanted to go to bed and sleep. Mandy's mother called their family nurse practitioner. She suggested letting her sleep for a few hours before coming in to her office where a psychologist also practiced. She wanted to examine Mandy and also have the psychologist evaluate her.

When Mandy woke up, the psychologist saw her and told her mother to take her home, feed her healthy foods, and help her get plenty of rest. She asked Mandy's mother to bring her back in two days, at which time Mandy still seemed in shock but wanted to talk more. In the meantime, Mandy found out that her friend was in the intensive care unit and in critical condition. She talked some about the accident but couldn't recall some of the specifics about what she saw. For instance, she didn't remember leaving the scene of the accident and going to school. The psychologist diagnosed her with acute stress disorder, which is not an uncommon diagnosis for someone such as Mandy who has been exposed to a traumatic event such as this accident. This diagnosis is given to people for up to a month after a trauma.

After a month Mandy told her therapist she was having nightmares about the wreck, and that she could vividly see the blood on Becky's face in the dream. She also started experiencing times when she was sitting in a classroom and had flashes of the accident come into her thoughts. Her parents were concerned because she wouldn't drive and insisted that her parents take the back streets and avoid the interstate when they drove. If it snowed, she worried that she would be involved in an accident. Even after her friend began to get better, Mandy continued to worry and be anxious. She rarely went to see her friend. Her mother said that she had trouble sleeping, eating, and really didn't want to be involved in her usual school activities. When these symptoms continued a month after the trauma it was diagnosed as PTSD. Therapy continued and a psychiatrist prescribed sertraline (Zoloft). In a few weeks she began to feel better and, with the help of her therapist, she began exposing herself to situations that reminded her of this accident.

℘

Criteria for Diagnosis

This diagnosis is seen when an individual "experiences or witnesses" a severe traumatic event and after a month fits the following criteria adapted from *DSM-IV-TR* (2000):

1. The traumatic event the child may be exposed to might involve death, serious injury, or a threat to either the child's or someone else's physical integrity.

2. The traumatic event in the child's life may result in feelings of fear, helplessness, or horror.

3. Some children respond to the event with disorganization or agitated behavior.

4. The child may experience intrusive thoughts or images that recall the traumatic event.

5. Children may play as a way of acting out the traumatic event.

6. The child may have a change in sleep habits because of recurring nightmares about the traumatic event. They may also have a hard time going to and staying asleep.

7. They may talk about feeling like they are reexperiencing the event. This may be in the form of hallucinations or dissociative flashbacks.

8. The child may experience physical reactions or psychological distress when exposed to either internal or external cues that remind them of the traumatic event.

9. They avoid activities or events that remind them of the traumatic event.

10. The child fears that they may not have a future.

11. The child may be unable to recall the events surrounding the trauma.

12. Their range of emotions seems to be restricted.

13. They show less interest in the normal activities of their daily life.

14. The child may be irritable and pessimistic and have decreased concentration.

15. They may startle easily.

16. The child may express guilt and sadness.

17. The child may have suicidal ideation or may have actually attempted suicide.

18. They may feel detached from others.

Post-traumatic stress disorder usually occurs within three months of the accident but may occur as late as several months or even years after the traumatic event. Terrorism, murder, rape, physical abuse, sexual abuse, accidents, and life-limiting diagnoses are just a few events that constitute traumatic events. If there are some dissociative responses, anxiety, and other symptoms (some of which are similar to the those for PTSD) within the first month after the traumatic event, then the diagnosis of acute stress disorder is made. Whether or not children develop this may have to do with their family supports, social supports, and early professional interventions. However, this is still being researched. Parents and teachers should watch for the child who is taking measures to self-medicate by alcohol or substance abuse along with other signs of anxiety and depression.

Obsessive-Compulsive Disorder (OCD)

☙ Joe's Story

Joe is an eleven-year-old boy who has been doing poorly in school for some time. Initially, Joe's doctor thought he had attention deficit hyperactivity disorder and treated him with the appropriate medication

(Ritalin). *It seemed to help for about the first three months, but then it no longer was effective. Joe continued to struggle in school and soon started showing signs of lower self-esteem. His teacher called to tell Joe's mother that he was not getting his schoolwork done during his study periods. He seemed sad to his teacher and continued to struggle with his grades. His teacher also observed that Joe spent a lot of time at his locker and they weren't sure why. His parents couldn't understand what was going on. They had always thought Joe had some odd habits. For instance, he always washed each contact lens for exactly three minutes per lens. When he went into the dining room, he would circle the table three times before sitting down to eat. There were also other things he did in terms of three times, such as wash his hands for three minutes, give his mother three kisses at bedtime, and check the zipper on his pants three times after he had gone to the bathroom. When Joe's parents described this to the school counselor, she thought it might be best if they shared the information with the boy's pediatrician. Joe's doctor thought maybe he had obsessive-compulsive disorder and sent him to the mental-health center for evaluation.*

ℰↃ

Criteria for Diagnosis

This is an example of when obsessive-compulsive behavior can interfere with the productivity of a child. More than likely, when Joe's teacher thought he was daydreaming, Joe was actually obsessing over something. *Obsessing* is when the child is thinking about something repeatedly and the *compulsions* are the behaviors that go along with obsessions. Children do not feel that these are within their control. Compulsions may manifest as things that are done in a certain alphabetical order, for a certain number of times, or for a specific amount of time. Behaviors like these are done for the purpose of controlling their anxiety. Often children who have OCD worry about germs, affecting how long they wash their hands, how they touch handles, and what they do if they shake someone's hand. When your child exhibits actions like these, they may be responding to obsessive anxiety. But here's the catch: sometimes when individuals become depressed, they may become obsessive-compulsive in an effort to take control of their life again. This is an example of when having some of the symptoms might be confused with having the disorder. Now let's look at the following criteria for the disorder. These criteria have been adapted from *DSM-IV-TR* (2000). They are:

1. The obsessions and compulsions take up at least one hour per day.

2. The child's OCD interferes with their daily home responsibilities, school routines, social activities, and friendships.

3. The obsessions are not simply real-life worries.

4. Other obsessions and compulsions may be performed in an attempt to control previous obsessions and compulsions.

5. The child's hands may be raw from washing them. Other signs may be an excessive amount of praying, counting, straightening, alphabetizing, placing things in order, and checking.

There are other mental-health diagnoses that should be considered by your doctors when your child presents with OCD. For example, Asperger's, tic disorders, eating disorders, and trichotillomania (hair pulling) are some other diagnoses that have an obsessive-compulsive quality to them. If your child has one of these disorders, the doctor will check for obsessive-compulsive disorder. On the other hand, if your child has obsessive-compulsive symptoms, the doctor will check for these other disorders. Be aware, they may occur together.

Asperger's Disorder

ଓ *George's Story*

The dark-haired, brown-eyed boy named George looked at the floor. After refusing to talk for about forty-five minutes, he spoke up. In a robotic type of speech he said, "You have a receding hairline and your eyebrows are dyed." His mother became embarrassed and said, "See, he's always saying something like that to people. He doesn't have any friends, and the teachers tell me they are uncomfortable around him."

George's teachers said that he was quite smart, but that his classmates didn't like him around them because he would say such odd things. He actually could communicate better with the faculty and staff than he could with his own classmates. His dad thought he wanted friends, but the kids just didn't like him. George had a very hard time relating to them because he was uncoordinated, and as a result he was rarely included in any playground games, much less team sports. He seemed sad to his parents much of the time. Their doctor agreed, but sensed there was something else going on with him. After a thorough evaluation, George was diagnosed with Asperger's disorder.

℘

Criteria for Diagnosis

Asperger's disorder could be thought of as form of social retardation. In addition to the social impairment, children with this condition also have repetitive patterns of behavior, symptoms that are often confused with those of OCD. These kids become obsessed and knowledgeable about one certain thing or a certain interest. For example, they may know every batting average of every major league player and from memory can give you these facts on any day. Some might become obsessed with a certain rock star and find out everything there is to know about that star. While these children can be very knowledgeable, they have very little ability to carry on a conversation with another person their own age. At times they can make conversation with adults, although this may be restricted since there is very little spontaneous response when talking to others. According to the *DSM-IV-TR* (2000), they differ from people with autism in that they don't have

* Delayed language development

* Delayed cognitive abilities

* Delays in "age-appropriate self-help skills"

* Delays in curiosity about their environment

Now let's look at the other characteristics that the *DSM-IV-TR* (2000) and other resources list as characteristic of Asperger's. They are the following:

1. Usually these children are referred to a psychologist for possible depression based on their poor nonverbal social skills and social isolation.

2. The child has poor same-age peer relationships.

3. They lack the ability to share mutual interests and enjoyment with other people.

4. These children lack in social reciprocity.

5. They exhibit motor movements such as hand flapping.

6. They become obsessed over certain parts of an object.

Kids with Asperger's may not receive the services at school that they need because of their lack of social skills. Often adults and peers in their environments take things these children say to them personally. Many times, the depression they experience is overshadowed by their inability to establish meaningful relationships, thus inhibiting them from receiving full mental-health service. These children need a full array of education and mental-health services in spite of what might be interpreted as a rather insulting nature.

Summary

This chapter has attempted to help you look at some of the other mental-health diagnoses your health professionals may consider if it seems that your child isn't responding to treatment for depression. In the event they don't consider an alternative explanation for your child's behavior, you may want to ask them about one of these diagnoses. Be familiar with what else may be causing your child to act the way they do. If nothing that I have discussed seems to fit and you don't feel you are getting anywhere with the present therapist's diagnosis then turn to other resources. You may want to ask for a second opinion or consult publications of the American Psychiatric Association and their excellent Web sites. There are other resources, which have been included in the Resources section of this book.

It may seem apparent after reading this chapter how many commonalities there are between many of the mental-health disorders. It should be no surprise, then, that it may take some time to get the correct diagnosis and treatment. One thing's for certain, the cognitive and behavioral strategies you've learned thus far are interventions that can be used for the majority of children's mental disorders. Start there and you'll be ahead in the game. The diagnosis will eventually surface.

In the next chapter, we'll be looking at some of the medications that can be used for depressive disorders and many of the other disorders as well. We'll also look at such things as compliance problems, common considerations when using medications, and interventions for the child who is unable to swallow pills.

Chapter 8

Medicating the Depression

ᕕ *Jill's Story*

Jill's parents sat in my office. "I just don't understand it, Dr. B. She's a zombie. We would rather have her irritable than the way she is now. Her teacher called and said Jill seems more depressed now than before she was treated. During class, Jill just sits there. The teacher says that sometimes she even sees Jill nodding off. I knew we shouldn't have started her on medicine, but we couldn't get in to see you or any other psychologist, so we decided to go ahead."

Jill is ten years old. For the past six months she has been extremely angry and tearful. Her grades have gone down to Cs from As and Bs. She doesn't want to try out for basketball this year even though she's always been the center for the team. Her parents worry because Jill goes directly to her room after school and goes to sleep. It's hard to get her up for dinner, which she feels is an interruption to her sleep. When Jill does eat, she can only get a little food down because she's lost her appetite. This was one of the earliest signs Jill's parents noticed because Jill had always been the child in the family who really loved to cook and eat. Now she doesn't do either one.

Jill's parents consulted their family doctor who decided Jill would probably feel better if she were started on an SSRI. After much deliberation, Jill's parents and doctor decided it was best if Jill was started on the antidepressant. She was told she would feel better in a few weeks. In the meantime, she just had to hang in there. Now the parents were faced with a daughter who seemed, in some ways, to feel worse than she did a month ago. The parents wondered whether the depression was worse or the medication just wasn't right for her. They hadn't been told what to

*expect from the medication, and Jill said she didn't want to hear any-
thing about it. If it were her choice, she wouldn't take the "stupid" drug.*

℘

Some Background about Medications

Taking medications is a big deal and should be treated as such.
Too often, I've found that people who are placed on medications
don't know the name of the medication, the dosage, the purpose,
or the side effects. Knowing these details can help keep them safe
when putting this foreign substance in their body. If you're considering giving medications to your child, it's important that you
are familiar with this information. This chapter will help you be
aware of information you need to know when giving your child
medications. It will also look at some of the more common medications used in childhood depression and the specifics about
those medications.

Have Drugs Been Tested for Children?

The most common question from parents is whether the drug
that is being used for their child has ever been tested on children.
Historically, more medications have now been tested for children
than ever in the past. Presently, clinical trials are being conducted
across the nation looking at the efficacy of antidepressants in children. Some trials have already concluded that these medications
are safe and effective in the treatment of childhood depression
(Weiner and Jaffe 1999). In the event there is lack of "experimental evidence," Kutcher (2000) stresses "clinical use of psychotropic
compounds at this time in the historic development of the knowledge base of this particular therapeutic mode may outstrip the
experimental evidence that exists to guide it" (243). In other
words, your doctor is making a decision based on an accumula-
tion of clinical knowledge about a specific medication for a specific clinical diagnosis. It should not be an uneducated guess. If
you are unsure about the use of a certain medication being used
on your child, ask your doctor what they have based their decision on. It is okay to ask—in fact, it's really your job. You need to
educate yourself about the "whys" of your doctor's decisions. If
the doctor finds this insulting, then you need to question if your

child is going to the right one. Competent doctors don't mind addressing questions.

Deciding If Medication Is Needed

You might wonder how your doctor and mental-health professional decide to pursue an evaluation for medication. There are criteria for deciding when that time arrives. Your doctor will probably begin considering medication if your child

* Has suicidal ideation (this may require hospitalization)

* Has homicidal ideation (this may require hospitalization)

* Refuses to get out of bed or has interrupted sleep patterns

* Refuses to eat

* Has significant weight loss or weight gain

* Refuses to go to school

* Has significant acting-out behavior

* Is not getting better despite ongoing therapy

* Is either struggling or failing in school

* Has family members who've been successfully treated with medication

* Is involved in alcohol or substance abuse

Make sure that when you see any of these warning signs, you go to a qualified physician to make the decisions regarding the necessity and choice of medication. To know whether your doctor is qualified you need to know where they have trained, how long they've trained, what the training has been, their specialty, and how long they have been in practice. You don't want to ask your eye doctor for a prescription for your child's depression. Also, it's best not to ask your good friend who happens to be a doctor for a prescription either. Your child needs a complete evaluation before these medications are started. Now let's look at what an evaluation consists of.

Defining an Evaluation

In chapter 2 I talked about what questions you should expect during the medical history done on your child. Notice I say "you should *expect*." I don't mean that it would be nice if these questions were asked—I mean these questions are the minimum that should be expected. Initially, your child should have a complete history taken, a physical, and the laboratory tests that would be indicated after this part of the assessment is completed. For instance, if your child presents with fatigue, weight gain, and feelings of depression, it would behoove your doctor to check your child's thyroid to rule out hypothyroidism before launching into pharmacological treatment. Concurrently, your child should be assessed by a mental-health professional who can do a complete psychological evaluation, including a family assessment, child assessment, school assessment (collecting grades, teachers' observations, and psycho-educational testing, if indicated), and observations of your child. Additionally, psychological testing may also be indicated as determined by your health professionals; tests should be conducted by a psychologist. Remember, it's important to do this complete assessment in order to establish a mental disorder and to delineate the target symptoms that are to be treated by the psychopharmacological treatment. According to Kutcher (2000), these targeted signs and symptoms should meet the following treatment criteria:

* Your child should be in significant distress.

* Those in the child's immediate environments should have significant distress as a result of the child.

* There should be an impairment of age-appropriate behavior.

* There should be a body of knowledge from the scientific literature supporting pharmacological intervention for your child's specific signs and symptoms.

* There are available psychological measures to evaluate the child before treatment and at different times after treatment begins to determine the progress of treatment.

In other words, when you and your doctor make a decision to treat your child with a psychopharmacological intervention, it should be done only after careful consideration and after certain treatment criteria are met. As much as possible, your child should be included in the decision to start medication. In the majority of cases, if your child has been given information, they will feel they are a part of the decisions. On the other hand, if the exchange of information is just between you and your child's doctor, it may result in your child feeling excluded and resentful. If your child doesn't feel like part of the team, there is a great chance that they might not cooperate in following the recommended treatment.

The use of pharmacological intervention should not be taken lightly. It should now be obvious why both your medical doctor and your psychologist or social worker should be a part of the evaluation while establishing these treatment criteria. Also, both specialties should be a part of the treatment.

If your doctor has decided to recommend a medication for your child's depression, you should expect your doctor to provide the necessary education. This education should be tailored for both you and your child. Remember, your child is the patient and needs to understand what's going on.

Physician's Education about the Treatment

The physician's education of the child and parents should include the following:

- The medical findings after the complete assessment

- The report of the psychological findings

- The report of the school's findings

- An explanation of your child's diagnosis

- The treatment alternatives for your child's disorder

- The physical causes of depression

- Why a pharmacological treatment needs to be considered for your child

- How a medicine is anticipated to correct what is troubling your child

- How other prescribed and over-the-counter medications your child is on will interact

- What alternative medications are available, and what the pros and cons are for each one

- How long it will take before the therapeutic effect begins to show for the different signs and symptoms (some minor changes may start as early as one to two weeks)

- How the medications work

- What to expect if serious adverse effects occur and what you should do

- The anticipated cost of the medication

- The difference between a generic and brand-name drug and whether your child can use a generic brand of the prescribed medication

- What the starting dosage will be and what the antici- pated maximum dosage will be

- An agreement not to discontinue the medication except under the supervision of your doctor

- How to get in touch with your doctor if concerns arise regarding the treatment of your child

- Your permission for your doctor to inform other team members regarding your child's evaluation and treatment

- An arrangement for therapy to start or to continue ongo- ing therapy

Getting Information about the Prescription

When you see your doctor, you should be prepared to take notes about your child's diagnosis and the medication prescribed. When your doctor gives you the prescription, ask about the name of the medication and why the doctor has chosen it. Look at the prescription together and have them go over what they have put on the prescription. Not only will this help you anticipate what your pharmacist should be doing with the prescription, but it helps your doctor check what they have written on the prescription. Sometimes pharmacists may misinterpret what your doctor has written on the prescription. For instance, if the prescription says to take the medicine once per day, it's helpful to have your doctor clarify those instructions. The doctor may want the medication taken at a certain time of day and the pharmacist may instruct you to do it another way. The doctor may say to take the medication before breakfast while your pharmacist says it needs to be taken on a full stomach. If you know what the doctor wants and the pharmacist advises you differently, then it's simple. Have them talk to each other and clarify exactly what you need to know and do. There are times your doctor might specify one medication, but when you get your prescription filled, you notice that the label has a different name. Who made the error? Or maybe it's not an error; you may have gotten the generic brand instead of the trade brand. At any rate, if you've done what I asked you to do at the very beginning when you got the prescription, then you will know if the medication is not right, if the dosage is off, or if there is a conflict between your doctor and pharmacist regarding the administration. It is your responsibility to check on these things. The "buck" stops with you.

Once you've gotten your child's medicine, it's important that you read the information provided to you about the medicine. I encourage you to do this with your child. They remember a lot of what has been talked about and really need to know any information regarding their medication. So read the label very carefully with your child, and compare it to the notes you have taken in your doctor's office. This is another cross-check. When you read the label, note the warnings it provides. These warnings are for that specific medication but don't take into consideration that your child may be on some other medication, either prescribed or over-the-counter (OTC). Remember, your pharmacist and doctor won't know what medications the child is taking unless you tell them. The interaction between all of the medications your child is on is potentially dangerous.

Here are some of the things you need to ask your pharmacist about your child's medicine.

* Which OTC medication is safe in combination with their depression medication.

* Whether any prescribed medications should not be taken with the presently prescribed medication.

* Any foods your child should avoid while being on a certain prescribed medication.

* Are they using a generic form of the medication for your child? Ask them to make sure they discuss this with your doctor. Generic may not be okay with your doctor.

* What are the specific instructions about taking the medication? This includes time of day, beginning dosage, and how to increase the dosage.

* What anticipated side effects are expected and what might be unanticipated side effects (adverse effects or lethal side effects) that would indicate an emergency?

* How to store the medications.

* Which side effects your child will experience and whether there are any that can only be detected through laboratory tests.

* What you can do for your child's side effects.

* Who you should call if you have questions about your child's medication.

Now let's talk about some issues of dosage.

Getting the Right Dosage

How your doctor decides what medication to prescribe and what dosage to use for your child's depression includes many variables. Once a medication is chosen, then your doctor will determine a dosage. Usually the dosage is based on what the literature recommends. Additionally, your doctor can get advice regarding your child's appropriate dosage from colleagues, schools of medicine, research centers for children's pharmacology, and telephone consultation (Kutcher 2000). Put simply, your doctor will base decisions about pharmacological interventions on information from a variety of professional resources.

Kutcher recommends that the lowest dose should be used to begin treatment for a child. This recommendation is made because, in some cases in which children are started on selective serotonin reuptake inhibitors (SSRIs), they may have adverse reactions because the initial dose is too high. According to Kutcher (2000) and Kastelic et al. (2000) a rule of thumb is "start low, and go slow" to prevent the adverse effects. Also, it is important for you to know that if adverse effects are going to occur, they will likely crop up three to four days after the pharmacological treatment has been started. Since your doctor has told you how long it's going to take before the therapeutic level is reached, you will know how long your child must wait for this level. This is important because often parents and children begin to become discouraged if they don't see the therapeutic effects take place immediately. Then you may begin pushing for an increased dosage. But remember, increasing your child's dosage prematurely may bring on adverse effects while still not achieving the therapeutic outcomes you want (Kutcher 2000). In some treatments, you may just have to be patient for the therapeutic changes to start.

In the event your child has had suicidal ideation, then it's important that small amounts of the medication be dispensed at a time. It's also important that you make sure that your child is actually swallowing their medicine so that they are not hoarding it to use for an overdose later. I had a mother tell me that she had been sure that her child took each dose she gave to him, only to find that he was actually pretending he put the medicine in his mouth. He would show his mother his empty mouth, then put the medicine in a hiding place. There the medicine accumulated over several months, while the child's signs and symptoms failed to improve. Fortunately, his mother found the stockpile before he could use it to overdose. I know your child may say you don't trust them if you ask to see them take and swallow their medicine. This can be difficult, but in the situation in which your child is talking about suicide, you may not be able to trust them. Don't be afraid to take a hard line on this, watching your child take and *swallow* the medicine. It may be the difference between illness and health—or even illness and death.

Now we'll look at an overview of the kinds of medication that may help your child.

Types of Medication for Your Child's Depression

The goal of treatment is to relieve your child's symptoms entirely, not just to reduce them (Shoaf et al. 2001). It is hoped that by doing that, it will be less likely that they will experience a reoccurrence as an adult (Shoaf et al. 2001). If this medication is going to work, it may take as long as twelve weeks for your child to achieve relief from their symptoms.

Selective serotonin reuptake inhibitors are considered the first drug of choice for children with depression. They include brands like Zoloft, Paxil, Prozac, Luvox, and Celexa. In the past, tricyclics have been used, but they were felt to have the potential for being harmful to your child's heart. If your child is placed on a tricyclic for any purpose, please remember that your child will need an EKG before the first dose of this medicine. There are other medications such as Wellbutrin that are also used for children, but for the purpose of this book, the SSRIs will be examined a bit more closely.

If your child is placed on an SSRI or another medication, remember to get all the necessary information about the drugs from your pharmacist and doctor. In addition, there are reference books available that can answer other questions you might have. For instance the *Physician's Desk Reference* (2003) is an excellent resource. You should keep in mind that this reference reports only information that the manufacturer reports about the drugs. But that can mean a lot of information, because the manufacturer reports everything that has ever been reported to them about adverse effects. It may be easier to sort through this type of information with your pharmacist. However, remember this resource is available for you.

What Is an SSRI?

SSRI is the abbreviation for the selective serotonin reuptake inhibitors. It does what its name says it does. If you recall, in chapter 3 I talked about there not being enough serotonin between the neurons in depression. An SSRI inhibits the neurons from taking up the serotonin so that there is more of it available in the space in between them. If there is more serotonin, then it's likely there will be a decrease in the depressive symptoms.

Common SSRIs

Trade name	Generic name	Dosing
Zoloft	sertraline hydrochloride	50 to 200 mg/day
Prozac	fluoxetine hydrochloride	5 to 40 mg/day
Celexa	citalopram hydrobromide	5 to 40 mg/day
Paxil	paroxetine hydrochloride	10 to 60 mg/day
Luvox	fluvoxamine maleate	50 to 300 mg/day

(*Nurse Practitioner's Drug Handbook* 2002; Wilens 2001)

Most of these medications come in tablet or capsule form, but if you prefer a liquid solution, ask your doctor about availability.

Your child's medication will likely be continued for six months to a year. However, if the doctor begins weaning the child from the medication and the symptoms return or worsen the dosage is likely to increase or go back to the maximum dosage used. Never stop the medication without consulting with the physician.

Adverse Effects of SSRIs

In a review of several research studies Kastelic et al. (2000) reported that SSRIs were generally well tolerated and had very few serious adverse effects. These adverse effects were reported as usually affecting the gastrointestinal system and the central nervous systems. According to Kastelic et al. (2000, 121), they are the following:

* Stomachaches

* Dyspepsia (heartburn)

* Nausea

* Anorexia

- Hyperkinesis (increase in motor activity)

- Agitation (restlessness)

- Tremor (nervous hands)

- Insomnia

- Somnolence (sleepiness)

- Headache

- Dizziness

There are instances when manic symptoms may appear. These symptoms may be caused by the medication or could be indicating bipolar disease in your child. Remember, depression is not an unusual presentation for bipolar disorder in a child. Looking for symptoms of possible bipolar disorder is just one reason that the prescribing doctor must follow your child closely. In any event, it's important that you report any manic symptoms to your doctor immediately. This usually results in a decrease or a change in your child's medication.

A very serious drug-induced allergic reaction called Stevens-Johnson syndrome can occur in your child. This is not necessarily seen in children on SSRIs but is seen in children on penicillin, sulfa drugs, and anticonvulsants. The reason I want to point this out to you is that sometimes when your psychiatrist has treated your depressed child they use more than one medication (like Depakote, a mood stabilizer). In this instance you must be aware of the Depakote's possible side effect. It starts with a rash and *must* be reported immediately to your doctor. Usually the rash disappears after discontinuing the drug, but if Stevens-Johnson syndrome is triggered, it needs emergency medical attention.

When Medication Isn't Working

The goal of therapy and pharmacological treatment is to help your child discover what is troubling them and to rid them of the physical signs and symptoms associated with the depression. At times, the therapy may result in the child succeeding in understanding the cause of their depression while they continue to suffer some physical symptoms. There are times when there is no change in the symptoms. What are some of the things your doctor will consider when the improvement is not what they'd anticipated?

- The diagnosis is not accurate.

- There is another diagnosis that coexists with the depression.

- The medication needs to be changed.

- The dosage of the medication needs to be changed.

- There is another prescribed medication, OTC medication, or herbal medicine that might be interacting with the antidepressant.

- The dosage was not increased gradually enough.

- There is a need of *augmentation,* which is when another medication is added to your child's medication to improve its response.

- There is an issue of nonadherence (your child is not getting the medication).

Most of these reasons are pretty self-explanatory, but I'd like you to be aware of some of the considerations your doctor or nurse practitioner should bear in mind if they think nonadherence (also referred to as noncompliance) is an issue (Rapoff and Barnard 1991).

- Your doctor has not included your child in the discussions of what is wrong and why there is a need for a medication.

- Your child has not been taught about how the medication works.

- Your child has not been taught how the medication should be taken.

- You have not been taught about the importance of the medication.

- You don't know how the medication works.

- You are not sure how to assist your child in taking the medication.

* Your child has not anchored their medication time to something in their routine that will remind them to take it (Kutcher 2000).

* There are side effects of the medication that the child did not anticipate.

* The medication side effects are intolerable.

* There is lack of parental supervision during drug-administration time.

* Your child or you sees little or no progress resulting from the medication.

* They have difficulty swallowing or taking the drug.

* The child feels you are forcing them into taking the antidepressant.

* Your child thinks that taking an antidepressant means that they are (or that you think they are) "crazy." They avoid this self-imposed label by not taking the medication.

* You can't afford the medication.

If your child is nonadherent, it's important to consider these things. Remember, there is a nonadherence rate of about 50 percent for medical regimens, usually for the reasons listed above. So if you think any of these reasons are valid talk to your doctor, psychologist, or nurse practitioner about correcting the ones they can help you correct. As far as you're concerned, the biggest one is making sure you are supervising your child when they take their medicine. After all, you would not put your school-aged children behind the wheel of a car, so why would you give them the sole responsibility to take their own medicine? Remember the example I gave earlier in this chapter about the child who stockpiled his antidepressants? Well, that was with supervision. Can you imagine what some children would do without supervision or with only a reminder? Work out something so that you know what your child is doing. Work out a reminder for yourself. Your child needs your support.

If the adverse effects are such that your child can't tolerate the medication, then talk to your pharmacist or your child's doctor or nurse practitioner to get treatments for these intolerable effects. If you can improve these, then the child is more likely to see the medication as helping rather than adding to the problem.

It's also important that you take your child for their follow-up appointments with the doctor and psychologist. Contact with these professionals is important for improved adherence. In the event the visit can't be done in person, then a phone call would be helpful.

Notice I have emphasized that the child should be seeing a mental-health professional as well as their medical doctor. We know that children will do better if they receive both medication and therapy then if they just receive medication. And, as I've said earlier, you don't want your child to perceive that a pill can make them feel and behave better. We want your child to know what the medication is capable of doing but also that they play a big role in helping themselves get better.

In the event that cost is a factor, then let your doctor know. Your doctor may have samples to help defray the cost or may be able to contact the pharmaceutical company to see if you qualify for assistance in obtaining the prescribed medication. Also, you may be able to obtain some help through contacting the pharmaceutical Web site www.phrma.org to get their suggestions for assistance in obtaining medications at a reasonable price.

Finally, I have pointed out that your child may have a problem taking a pill. This is not unheard of for most ages. Here are some suggestions that might help.

- If the medication has a bad taste, then coat the tongue with something like chocolate syrup.

- If the pill catches in the throat, make sure your child drinks something before to lubricate the throat and esophagus.

- If your child needs something to transport the medication, put the pill or tablet into a food like jelly, peach syrup, applesauce, or ice cream.

- If your child's gag reflex is getting triggered, try having them use a straw when taking a pill.

- If your child says that it feels like the pill gets caught in their throat, then try a warm liquid with or after taking the pill.

* If you are mixing your liquid medicine into another liquid, ask your pharmacist whether you're using the appropriate liquid base.

In the event the problem has to do with learning how to swallow a pill or capsule, try using the tips I provide below. If your child still has difficulty swallowing pills, ask your psychologist or social worker to help you with teaching your child this technique or to refer you to someone who can teach your child. Here are some procedures adapted from a study from Blount et al. (1984) and developed by the students and staff of the Pediatric Psychology section of The University of Kansas Medical Center between 1985 and 1999.

1. Buy cake decorating sprinkles of all sizes, from the very little ones up to sprinkles that approximate the size of your child's pill. This may be the size of a Tic-Tac. The idea is to have incremental sizes of pill substitutions starting very small and advancing to the size and shape of the pill that needs to be taken. Do not use vitamins as the substitution. Some vitamins can be toxic if taken in an overdose. Cake sprinkles and candy work well as long as your child does not get the idea that pills are like candy, though this isn't usually a problem with a school-age child. It's more likely to occur with a younger child, so you must take special care to ensure they don't confuse the two. One doctor used different sizes of beans with his younger child so that his child was not confused about medicine being candy.

2. Have your child look at themselves in the mirror so they can see what they'll look like when taking a pill. I have discovered some children will tilt their head back to swallow, while others will tuck their chin down to swallow.

3. Begin with just using the glass with water in it. Have your child practice the motion of taking a pill. Go ahead and show them how you would do it to model the technique. Have them pretend to take a pill, swallowing only water, while watching themselves in the mirror.

4. Next, start with the smallest cake sprinkles and have your child place one on the back of the tongue and follow with

water. In order to build a little incentive in this you might offer your child something they can earn when they are successfully taking his medication. Always be positive about your child's attempts and never punish them for their failures unless they refuse to cooperate. Then time-out strategies will need to be initiated. If your child can swallow the first sprinkle successfully two times, then give them a point.

5. Now go to the next size of the training pill substitution. Role model this size for your child and repeat the first step involved with chasing the pill substitution with water.

6. If at any time your child gags go back to the previous size they were successful with and repeat that with water. Always end on a positive note.

7. Keep working at this until your child can swallow a pill-sized substitute.

8. This procedure may take from a few hours to a few days.

Always focus on the positives, paying attention to your childs attempts, not failures. Praise for the attempts but provide tokens for two successful attempts in swallowing the pill substitution. When using a token system, make sure your child can earn chips or points for these two successes at each step of learning pill taking. The number of points your child is able to earn should be predetermined. These points or chips can be exchanged for predetermined backup reinforcers. (See chapter 5 for additional guidance on the token system.)

If you don't want to use a token system, then try a grab bag. This is a bag filled with slips of paper that have one of three things written on them (time with a parent; time doing something like, TV watching; or a small inexpensive object like gum, baseball cards, or barrettes). These slips can be exchanged after two successful attempts taking one of the pill substitutions.

Remember, learning the technique of pill taking doesn't have to be done in one sitting. Your child can get to a step of success and then practice that for a while, earning some points for that practice. The time for this practice also needs to be predetermined so that it's not used for avoidance.

Hopefully these suggestions will help with improving the adherence of your child to the prescribed pharmacological intervention. In the event it remains a problem it should be one of the things your child works on with a psychologist.

Summary

We've been looking at what goes into a medical assessment that will determine if your child would benefit from and tolerate a pharmacological intervention. I've also tried to stress the importance of your doctor including you and your child in the explanations of their findings and the options they feel you have in order to help your child. Careful, age-appropriate explanations are encouraged for your child so that they can feel part of the decisions regarding treatment. If your child feels excluded, they may resist treatment. They may feel they are being forced to take a medicine against their will. They can interpret this as being disempowered or may see it as the adults in their life telling them they are crazy.

We've also looked at SSRIs as the first drug of choice for childhood depression and what should be expected as a treatment outcome. In the event that your child has adverse reactions to medication, you now know something about the causes and remedies. We've also discussed issues of nonadherence and the nitty-gritty of pill taking.

The next chapter will look at some life experiences in which your child will experience sadness and depression. These experiences result in grief for most kids, and the chapter will help you understand your child as they go through these changes and experience loss. Loss, for the purpose of the next chapter, will be defined as parental separation, divorce, or the loss of a parent.

Chapter 9

Grief and Children

ಸಾ Kenny's Story

Kenny sat with his mother and father in my office. They had told him the previous night that they were going to get a divorce. They were concerned because he didn't say much. He just asked if he would see each of them and whether he would have a bedroom at each of their houses. They reassured him that he would see both of them but they let him know that they hadn't worked out the schedule yet. In the meantime, he would alternate weeks with each parent. In a few weeks a more definite visitation schedule would be established. Each parent looked exhausted but it was nothing compared to the exhaustion Kenny exhibited.

Both parents were irritable with each other the day of the appointment, but nothing like they had been for the six months prior to their decision to get a divorce. Nevertheless, they felt sure that they had kept their disagreements from their only child. They talked in their bedroom. They discussed their differences when he was at school, with friends, or in bed. They had no reason to believe that Kenny knew that anything was going on between them.

Kenny's teacher had called several times during the past two months to say that Kenny seemed distant, almost depressed. His grades had gone down to Ds. He refused to work at school and many times would not turn his assignments in. This baffled his parents because they would ask him if he had homework, and he always said no.

Kenny's parents were both professionals. Every weekday afternoon his mother would call to see if he had gotten home okay. He was not alone because he had a baby-sitter with him until one of his parents got home, often as late as eight o'clock. But in spite of his baby-sitter's efforts, Kenny still felt alone. He was worried about his parents. They looked and acted different to him. He surmised that they were having marital problems because he would hear them argue after he had gone to bed. He noticed his mother had been crying many mornings and his Dad would leave before he got up to go to school. He wondered what he had done to make them want to fight like this.

Kenny became sadder and sadder. He began to think that if he got sick or flunked out of school that it would make his parents stay together. After all, they had always come together when he'd been in trouble before. Now maybe they would see it was necessary to stay together to help their son pass this year in school.

ℰℑ

Divorce As the Choice

Over half of the marriages in the United States end in divorce. Children are aware that many of their peers live in these situations, and so when their parents have a disagreement they often wonder if it will end in divorce. Many times when parents are having problems they make genuine attempts to keep their disagreements in private, so as not to worry their children. Unfortunately, those attempts are rarely successful. Your children have lived with you for all of their lives and can sense it as soon as something is out of kilter. Parents' behaviors, dispositions, and routines change when they are faced with marital problems. Who knows these characteristics better than your own child? Kids will tell me long before parents do that something is going on in the marriage. Their parents will deny it, but in my experience, many of these children's concerns turn out to be true.

I guess what I'm trying to say is, please take your arguments outside the home. There are no secrets from your child. Remember, they can hear you blink.

Once the Decision Is Made to Divorce

When you have decided to get divorced, then your first obligation is to tell your children. I would advise you to do this before you separate. This gives the children an opportunity to anticipate that one of their parents will no longer live with them in their home. It also gives the children the opportunity for some ongoing interactions with both parents. They'll have the chance to ask questions as they arise rather than waiting for the answers. Children do better if they can obtain information in small amounts so that they can realize exactly what is going on. Because this is a crisis for your family, your child may not absorb and remember exactly what is told them. You may find yourself repeating some of the information, and they may even deny what you have told them. If the parents stay together for a few days after the divorce announcement, it will allow both of you to answer some questions as they become evident.

You may want to spare your child the whole truth about the divorce, telling them instead that you're just getting a separation. You may feel this will help them adjust better to your divorce. The fact is, it's better for you to tell your children the truth. This doesn't mean you have to give them all the details about what led to the divorce. For instance, your child does not have to know whether an affair occurred, unless they are likely to hear it from their friends. Your child will be angry if they have been lied to and will be less likely to believe you about subsequent information. Also, remember that your child's wonderful imagination can be pretty harmful when it comes to filling in all the details about something like your divorce. They can deal with the truth. Be honest with your child.

How Do I Tell My Child?

It's important for both parents to tell the child about the divorce. They need to know that, in spite of you being separated and divorced, you can still come through together for them. If only one parent tells the child, it's likely that they will view the absent parent as the "bad guy." You are still your child's parents and will be together when it comes to rearing them. It is of the utmost importance that you get this message across to your child. You must strive to put your differences aside and make sure you act on this message. Your child needs both of you as parents.

If you can't tell your child what is happening as two parents because you disagree on what to say or one parent is absent, then I would encourage you to get professional help. Initially, you should decide what you're going to tell your child and who is going to tell them. I would also encourage you to handle any significant anger between the two of you, either alone or with professional help, before talking to your child. You can even tell your child what's happening in the presence of the therapist. Follow-up appointments should be made to determine visitation decisions and any other decisions that relate to your children. At times, your children may need their own appointments with a mental-health professional to help them adjust to this change in their life.

Your Child's Reaction to Divorce

There is great diversity in how children react to their parents' divorce. In any event, there is always some degree of devastation. This stems from a number of variables that include the following:

* The age of the child

* Gender of the child (males having the most behavioral problems; girls struggling more in adolescence)

* The amount of controversy in the home prior to the divorce

* The degree of support they receive from extended family and friends

* The quality of the relationship with the custodial and the noncustodial parent

* Whether the life of the child changes significantly (for instance, a decrease in financial status or change in schools)

* If it effects the child's relationship with their peer group

* If discipline remains effective and consistent

Regardless of these variables, your child will likely react to your divorce with some symptoms of grief. How much you share with them and prepare them for the divorce can do much to lessen the intensity of their grief reactions. Initially, your child may be very shocked, unless they were aware of the problems all along. Other times your child may plead with you to not get a divorce. They may beg one of their parents to please stay. Even being prepared for the inevitable will not lessen the intense sadness and anger your child is likely to feel once you disclose your divorce plans. How long it takes for them to resolve this grief reaction varies. In some cases, it may never totally be resolved.

Children tend to feel quite guilty over the divorce and search for personal reasons for how they may have caused it. Even after you've let them know that they had no part in why their parents are getting divorced, your child is likely to continue to question this.

In many ways, your child may hold hope that someday you will get back together with their other parent. Sometimes children act out and get in trouble in an attempt to bring their parents back together. This hope can be held for years and becomes evident when your child becomes quite sad and angry when you decide to marry again.

Children going through a divorce may not only show these behaviors of sadness and anger but also be irritable, oppositional, and aggressive, and show regression behaviors and grief behaviors. Teachers may note that your child's grades decline and report that your child acts out in the classroom, or they may see your child as more sad and insecure. Whatever the reaction is, you must attend to your child and help them deal with the inevitable.

Your Child's Questions

Your child will have many questions on how this divorce pertains to them. As I have said earlier, they will also want to know what part they played in your getting divorced. The following are some questions you might anticipate:

* What did they do to cause this divorce? Your child will look back at their own behavior and question if things such as their poor grades, behavior problems, or a refusal to do their chores have caused you to get a divorce. Even if they don't have any problems, they will wonder what they might have done.

* Will their friends still like them? Children will wonder what their friends will do when they hear that their parents are getting a divorce.

* Will what happened to their friends happen to them, too? Your child may have been exposed to some peers who were sad and acting out because of things their parents did after their divorce. Your child may

automatically think that is what's going to happen to them. Remember, kids with sadness and depression often have automatic irrational thoughts.

* Where will they live, and will they have their own room at both residences?

* When will they go to each parent's home?

* Will both parents be involved in their school and extra-curricular activities?

* Who else knows about this situation?

* Do their parents plan to tell people about the divorce, and who will tell them?

* When are other people, such as the school, going to be told about the divorce?

* Are they going to stay in the family home or will they have to move?

* Will there be changes in the family's financial status?

These questions need to be anticipated and answered as quickly as possible by both parents. If children are left with their questions, it's more likely they will have a difficult time adjusting to the divorce.

Rules for Divorce

There are certain rules for both parents to adhere to when a divorce occurs. They are the following:

* Reassure your children that you both love them. Tell them that no matter what happens between you as a couple, it will never change how you feel about them.

* Your children need consistent discipline at both homes. I would advise you to make every attempt to make discipline consistent in and between each home. If you can't come to an agreement with the other parent about a discipline issue, then make sure you remain consistent in your home and that you base your discipline on behavioral principles. Try to remain positive in your home.

- Do not make your children your messengers. If you have something to say to their other parent, take care of it yourself. It is not your child's job to do this.

- Your child is not your spy. At no time should you ask your child what your former spouse is doing, who your former spouse is dating, or whether your former spouse seems sad.

- Don't quiz your child about everything they do with your former spouse.

- Don't try to get your child to take sides in the event you are fighting with your former spouse. I'm hoping you didn't do this before your divorce, and you shouldn't do it now.

- If you do have the tendency to continue to fight with your former spouse, try not to fight in front of your children.

- If your child is talking to their other parent on the phone, don't listen in on the other extension, and don't hang around to hear what your child is saying. What they say to each other is not your business.

- If you find your child crying about the divorce, don't discourage it. Watch for the signs of depression that we have discussed earlier in this book.

- It is okay for your child to see you crying as long as they also see you stop crying and carry on normal activities. If you are suffering from depression, get professional help.

- Make sure you tell your child's teacher and counselor about your situation so that they are available to support your child and to watch how your child adjusts.

- Tell your friends about the divorce so that you can clear up any rumors regarding it.

- Encourage your child to share any scuttlebutt they've heard from friends so that you can clarify what is true and what is simply rumor.

- When talking to your child, always speak of your former spouse with respect. Remember, your ex is also their parent. If you speak negatively about them, your child will begin to resent you.

- If there is a third party involved with the divorce, do not become overly anxious to introduce your children to that person. Your child needs to adjust to your divorce first, and respecting your child's needs is particularly important right now.

- If you have major concerns about your finances and how you are going to make it after the divorce, you can let the child know there may be some changes coming, but don't burden them with the details or your fears. They have plenty to do in adjusting to the divorce, and shouldn't have to worry about adult matters like this.

- Eventually you may have to tell your child about a number of big changes that stem from the divorce (for example, you need to move or one of the parents who used to stay at home now has to work). Give your child time to adjust to one change at a time, if you are able.

- As much as possible, keep your child's life the same. For example, as much as you are able, keep your child in the same neighborhood, at the same school, and in the same home.

- Give your child time to express to both parents how the divorce has affected their life.

- Each parent should give each child in the family one-on-one time each day that they are with them.

- Refrain from leaving your child with a baby-sitter immediately after your divorce, even if you feel the urge to date right away. I know it's important for you to feel better about yourself after a divorce, but if you leave your children too early they might feel abandoned. It can be a set-up for your children to have major problems.

- Allow other family members, friends, and church members to support you. As with any other grief states, individuals do better if they have good support systems.

- If you are the noncustodial parent, try your best not to only play the "good guy" role, leaving the other parent to be the only one to set limits and impose discipline.

- Both parents need to attend your child's school meetings and performances.

- Both parents need to attend your child's sporting events.

- Have a designated adult (not one of the parents) your child can talk to if they have concerns regarding either of their parents' behavior.

Red Flags

I have described some of the reactions children have to hearing that their parents will be getting a divorce. I also have suggested guidelines that can help you manage this situation so that you can minimize these reactions. But what happens if a child does not adjust to the divorce over a period of time? A child who can't seem to move through their grief is at risk for depression and should be watched. Here are the red flags you should be looking for. They are

- Changes in eating habits (increase or decrease)

- Weight gain or weight loss

- Changes in sleeping habits (insomnia, waking in the middle of the night, nightmares, and early morning awakenings)

- Increase in fears (like separation anxiety)

- Decline in grades

- Acting-out behavior

- Irritability

- Oppositional behavior

- Withdrawal from friends and social activities

- Decreased concentration

- References to death, either through verbal interactions, notes, or pictures

If you see any of these red flags in your child then get them to a mental-health professional. Many of these sustained grief reactions can result in major depression.

Special Considerations

In the event abuse existed in the marriage or was what led to the divorce, I suggest that you work with a professional who can guide you and keep you and your children safe. If there has been child abuse as well as spousal abuse, then your child must also get into therapy. Obviously, the professional will have to report child abuse to authorities in order to protect your child. Don't hide this from the professional.

ଜ *Kelly's Story*

Nine-year-old Kelly sat on the bed and held her mother's hand. "Please don't go Mama," she said. Her mother looked up at her as a tear trickled down her right cheek. "I'll be in heaven with your grandfather." "Will you look down at me and help me with my math?" Her mother smiled and nodded yes.

Kelly wondered what she had done to make her mother ill. She hadn't told anyone of these fears, but she was sure there must have been something. Maybe it was when she wouldn't do her homework or when she refused to do her chores. If only she had done those things. "Maybe if I'm really good now, then Mama will get well," she thought. "I wonder what will happen if my dad gets sick, too. Who would take care of me and Nathan?"

Her days were spent trying to do better in school. Her room was organized, unlike she had ever kept it before. Her books were alphabetized. Her clothes were arranged by color. She said exactly five prayers every night, no more and no less. She worried that she would bring germs home from school and infect her daddy. She washed her hands frequently, sometimes up to thirty times a day. Her hands were raw. She refused to kiss her dad because she might give him something and then he would be sick like her mother.

After several months of illness, Kelly's mother died, leaving her husband, Kelly, and four-year-old Nathan. Kelly cried initially but soon started acting as though nothing had happened. She continued with her ritualistic behaviors but otherwise acted as if nothing was wrong, going back to playing with her dolls, drawing, and playing outside. Her dad believed that this behavior was not normal.

ଜ

Circumstances Affecting Reaction

There is evidence that children who have always been protected from exposure to death-related experiences have problems with coping with death experiences later in their childhood and even as adults. It is a natural phenomenon for children to be inquisitive about death. Think about those times when your child has wondered what happens to their pet when it dies. They express sadness and the need to hold a service for their pet in the backyard. Some parents think this is strange or something they need to protect their child from. The fact is, these experiences begin to teach your child that death is a natural part of the life cycle. Even kids' books, movies, or plays that deal with death can help them learn this lesson. Unfortunately some protected children confront the death experience for the very first time when they lose a parent or sibling from illness, terrorism, war, or an accident. How devastating this can be!

Notice I did not say this is their first loss. Children proceed through their lives from the newborn period on through adolescence experiencing loss. If these developmental stages are accomplished successfully and in a healthy fashion, then children learn they can survive devastating loss. In cognitive terms, they have evidence that they can cope with loss and stand it.

Children's reaction and ability to cope with a death depends on a variety of other things as well. These include the following:

* The child's age determines how the child conceptualizes death. The young child sees death as reversible, while the seven- to ten-year-old will conceptualize death as permanent and irreversible. Adolescents will also see it as permanent but will look at it in more abstract terms.

* Whether the death was anticipated or unexpected.

* The type of preparation the child has had for the death

* The type of relationship the child had with the person.

* Whether there were unresolved differences the child had with the person.

* Whether there were unmet promises made to the child by the deceased person.

- Circumstances surrounding the actual death will determine how the child copes with it. For instance, the change of the physical appearance of their loved one will alter the way they cope.

- How long it takes the individual to die. In many instances a prolonged dying process can be harder on the child.

- What role the dying individual had in this child's life. For instance, if the child is losing their mother and she is a stay-at-home mother who did all of the household chores, there will be a significant change in the roles of everyone in the home.

- Whether the person dies in the child's home or in the hospital. Many times this varies depending on whether they think their children can handle their loved one dying at home.

- The role the child had in caring for the deceased loved one.

- The child's mental-health history.

- How many sources of support the child has (for instance the extended family, church family, friends, professionals, and school personnel).

- If the child is with the loved one when they die.

- If the child is kept among their family and home environment after the death or is sent away from the home.

- The child's ability to have their basic needs met and whether their caregivers are able to continue regular routines and provide consistent, effective discipline.

- The child's understanding of the cause of the death.

- The child's ability to discuss the cause of death and the dying process with adults.

- Whether the child is able to share their loss with other children their age who have experienced similar losses.

- The child's participation in the planning of the funeral or memorial service.

As you can see, there are a number of variables that will play a part in a child's reaction and coping with a loved-one's death. Now let's look at the grief reactions in the school-age child.

Grief Reactions and Bereavement of Children

Children have unique responses to the loss of a loved one, reactions that are different from those of adolescents and adults. Remember, these responses vary depending on the circumstances in the preceding list. Also, you need to know that there is no time limit on bereavement. The intensity may change over time, but the bereavement may be chronic. Children who lose a parent early in life may be likely to suffer from depression in later years.

Another word about how long grief will last: For whatever reason, people often think children should be over their grief in three months or a year. I know a teacher who told a child that he should just get over his father's death and get on with life. This was five months after the child's father had died. Unfortunately, that teacher was obviously unaware of the nature of the grief process. In the case of an unexpected death, actual bereavement may not even start until months after the death because the survivors are in shock. Even in an expected death, the child may not feel grief until several months into the first year. Either way, the three-month mark tends to very difficult for those close to the deceased because this is when most people outside the family have completed their grief, often leaving those still affected to grieve on their own. The loss of support at this time can be devastating.

Each family member may also grieve at a different rate. When one seems to have resolved some of the grief, another member may be in their heaviest part of it. In some ways this is good—it may enable members to support each other more effectively. When your child is grieving they need the support of the parent, who may be fatigued with their own grief. At times, the parent will have very little energy to put toward supporting their own child. That's why this is the time to have your extended family and friends available to support your child. It's also time to get professional help to counsel you through your child's and your bereavement.

Make every effort to resist judging your child if they have gotten back into their normal activities very soon after their loved one's death. Children learn to cope by playing and getting back into normal activities. This isn't abnormal and should not be looked at as your child forgetting the loved one. It's actually just the opposite.

Make sure school personnel are kept apprised about what is going on. In some instances the teacher may make this a learning experience for the classroom and tell them what has happened and what they can expect from their classmate. Children need to be advised on how to support their friend and then be allowed to do something as a class to show this support during the time of early grief. I would recommend that the child return to school a few days after the death so that the routines can be reinstated.

Finally, grief reactions do not have to come in a certain order and they do not all have to be present. I present the common reactions to grief in a linear way, but some may come sooner or later in the process than you might expect. I sometimes see these responses happening all at once and unexpectedly, like a tidal wave. Children should be warned about these feelings so they are not fearful if one of them hits unexpectedly. So often they think they are "crazy."

Here are the reactions to grief you might expect in your child.

Early Reactions

* Shock (depending on the circumstances of the death)

* Numbness

* Sadness

* Crying

* Calling to or searching for the lost loved one

* Anger

* Fear ("Will I die of the same thing? Who is going to take care of me?")

* Denial

* Guilt ("What did I do to cause this?")

- Confusion
- Fatigue
- Physical complaints
- Nightmares
- Loss of appetite
- Bargaining

Later Reactions

- Physical complaints
- Decreased attention span
- Sadness
- Loneliness
- Visual and auditory hallucinations
- Dreams about the lost loved one (this is usually later for the family members and earlier for friends)
- Sleep disturbances
- Eating disturbances

At-Risk Behaviors

- Acting-out behavior
- Oppositional behavior
- School avoidance
- Declining school grades
- Refusal to do school work
- Multiple illnesses

High-Risk Behaviors

- Signs of depression (see the characteristics listed for depression in chapter 1)
- Aggression
- Signs of suicidal ideation

* Possible alcohol and substance abuse

If you have lost a loved one and are concerned about your child, make sure you get some professional to help to guide you through this period. Also remember that your child may do better if they are able to have some of the personal belongings of the loved one. Such things as pictures, jewelry, and clothing may offer some support to your child. Do not change the personal environment too quickly. Also, if the child wants to visit the cemetery, that's just fine, but don't force it until they want to. You will know when the time is right—just listen to your child.

If you have suspicions that the grief is looking abnormal, then seek advice. Your judgment may not be at its best because of your own grief. Be realistic with yourself and *get help*. Professionals can help you determine if your child needs additional help.

Summary

We've been exploring children's experience of loss as it relates to divorce and the death of a loved one. The things that have been discussed as they relate to these losses have common threads and can be applied to other losses a child might experience. For instance, your child needs to be told what is going on, rather than leaving the information to their imagination. Also keep your eye on your child, especially if they are getting into a lot of self-blame for what has happened. It's common for the child to try to figure out in some way who is to blame, and usually the child will look to themselves for the answers. Remember, children go through grief but may do some of their coping through play, which may be misunderstood as the child not caring. Children seek normalcy in their life. Play is a way to help them feel more normal and secure. Finally, they need regular routines and effective, consistent discipline at this unsettled time.

Next we're going to wrap things up. I'll share with you my final thoughts on rearing children and preventing and identifying depression.

Chapter 10

Final Thoughts

෨ *Christie's Story*

Christie beamed and said, "I just came by to let you know that I made the honor roll and I haven't missed one day of school yet." Her mom chimed in, "Yes, and she doesn't even argue with us anymore."

I had seen Christie a year ago for depression. Before seeing me, she'd been seen by her pediatrician multiple times for chronic complaints of headaches. The pediatrician finally sent her to the neurologist, who ruled out a brain tumor. He told her to go back to school. But Christie just couldn't get herself up in the mornings. Her mother wasn't sure how you could force an eleven-year-old to go to school.

She took Christie back to the pediatrician who decided that she was depressed. She was started on an SSRI and sent to me to begin cognitive therapy. After about two months, Christie started getting the sparkle back in her eyes. She was attending school and her teacher had tailored Christie's assignments until she started feeling better, then it was back to the normal load. Earlier in the year, Christie had missed several assignments. At that time the teachers got together to determine what the minimum was she had to do in order to learn the concepts but not feel overwhelmed. The school, the doctor, her parents, Christie, and I all worked as a team to get Christie caught up and to help her begin feeling better. After six months, Christie was back to her old self. She was involved in sports, social events, and was doing much better at home and in school accomplishing her responsibilities. She no longer saw me but did remain on her SSRI.

෨

Your Child Can Get Well

Often parents are very pessimistic regarding whether their child can get better. They question their own abilities to evaluate their child. If you begin feeling this way, please ask your doctor or school personnel if they have seen the same changes you have. It's important to get your child evaluated as soon as possible. Remember, early intervention for childhood depression lessens the likelihood of it reoccurring in adolescence or adulthood.

You Are Your Child's Advocate

It can be a pretty lonely job to be a child in the best of circumstances. A child who happens to be struggling emotionally needs to know that someone is in their corner. You, as your child's parent, must be that person. If children can't rely on their parents at home, then who can they rely on? Unfortunately, they will then turn to peers who may not be the best influence. You need to try to spend some extra time with your children so that they know you are there, what the rules are, and what the consequences are when they break those rules. They must know what to expect. That's not asking too much.

Be Knowledgeable

It is crucial that you become knowledgeable about the emotional problems of childhood. Raising a child without a thorough understanding of childhood emotional problems is like driving a car with a blindfold on. Take the blindfold off and be aware of what is going on with your child.

Besides being aware of these potential emotional problems, it's also important to know what can be done about them. Knowing medical, psychological, and educational interventions is essential for helping your child during this time of distress. It is the main focus of this book to help you gain this knowledge. Without these interventions, it's likely that your child may not get well. Ignorance is not bliss.

Being Positive Is the Key to Good Self-Esteem

Children will try to get attention any way they can. The best kind of attention to offer is recognition for positive behaviors. If they don't get attention for what they've done right, then they'll get your attention another way. Usually they'll try some kind of inappropriate behavior, because that is guaranteed to get attention immediately, whereas it sometimes takes much longer to get attention for doing something good. Based on what you have learned about behavioral principles, which behavior is more likely to keep occurring? By turning your attention to their positive behavior, you'll encourage more of the same. This positive dynamic is essential for your child's self-esteem.

Parents Need Help, Too

I am often amazed by how quick parents are to blame problems in a family on their child. After reading this book, you now know that your child may be reflecting your problems. I agree that your child needs their own mental-health professional, but maybe you do, too. If you have cholesterol problems, aren't you going to look at your whole cardiovascular status rather than just your blood? Won't you exercise as well as watch what you eat? Well, the same is true in a family. If your child is having a problem, then a thorough evaluation needs to be done to determine what else might be going on in your family. All of the problems need to be addressed in order for your child to begin getting well. If this doesn't happen, your child may have problems come up over and over again.

Medications Can Help

Many parents are initially unwilling to put their child on a medicine. I've heard many reasons for this, but most boil down to misunderstanding what medications do. I agree that in a lot of instances, medications are not needed. A change in parenting and some help in school often suffices. But when that isn't enough, you may need to make yourself knowledgeable about medications and what they can do. The message to your child should be that a pill won't make them well. It will just change the brain chemistry enough so that they can begin learning ways to make themselves well. Your child will have to get to school themselves, the pill won't do that. They will have to change their thoughts, the pill won't do that. They will have to eat, the pill won't do that. The pill will help, but the work resides with the child. Empower your child.

If the Diagnosis Doesn't Seem Right

There are times when the diagnosis of depression is either slow in evolving or is not the correct diagnosis. This doesn't necessarily mean that your doctors aren't good. It means that a lot of diagnoses start out looking like one thing and end up being another. Also, it could mean that depression is not the only diagnosis. The important message here is that if you don't see an improvement in your child's behavior, ask your professionals about it. If this insults them, then you're going to the wrong professional.

Devastating Life Events

Unfortunately, life is not always good and easy for children. Some children have to face loss at a very young age. All too often these losses can be devastating, not only because of what they represent to the child, but also because of how these events are handled by the child's parents.

Many parents try to protect their kids by keeping them in the dark about details. But children need to be in the know about what is going on in their family. They will find out in their own way. If you have lied to them regarding what's happening in the family, they may have trouble trusting you in the future. Tell your child what is going on and prepare them for the inevitable. Like everything else in life, if a child is prepared for what is happening in the family or to a friend, they can handle it. It doesn't mean they won't grieve, but grief is a healing process of its own. By helping your child anticipate what will happen, you'll enable them to negotiate the future more easily.

Final Words

Thank you for allowing me to share my thoughts. Throughout this book, I've tried to speak my mind, reflecting my passion for helping good parents such as you. The fact that you are reading books about childhood tells me just how good a parent you really are. Keep up your search for answers and you will enable yourself to be the best possible parent you can. You cannot ask any more of yourself than that.

Resources

Books

Emswiler, Mary Ann, and James P. Emswiler. 2000. *Guiding Your Child through Grief.* New York, Bantam.

Feinberg, Linda Sones. 1996. *Teasing: Innocent Fun or Sadistic Malice?* Far Hill, NJ: New Horizon Press.

Nolte, Dorothy Law, and Rachel Harris. 1998. *Children Learn What They Live.* New York: Workman Publishing.

Weyburne, Darlene. 1999. *What to Tell the Kids about Your Divorce.* Oakland, CA: New Harbinger Publications.

Wilens, Timothy E. 2001. *Straight Talk about Psychiatric Medications for Kids.* New York: Guilford Press.

Hotlines and Telephone Numbers

800-SUICIDE (24 hours a day, 7 days a week

800-THERAPIST (therapist location information)

Organizations

American Academy of Child and Adolescent Psychiatry
3615 Wisconsin Ave. NW
Washington, DC 20016-3007
202-966-7300
www.aacap.org

American Association of Marriage and Family Therapists
112 South Alfred St.
Alexandria, VA 22314-3016
202-452-0109

American Association of Suicidology
   Suite 310
   4201 Connecticut Ave. N.W.
   Washington, D.C. 20008
   202-237-2280
   www.suicidology.org

Depression and Bipolar Support Alliance
   730 N. Franklin St.
   Suite 501
   Chicago, IL 60610-7204
   800-826-3632

The Medicine Program (patient assistant information)
   573-996-7300

National Hospice Organization
   1901 North Moore St. #901
   Arlington, VA 22209
   703-243-5900

National Information Center for Children and Youth with
   Disabilities
   P.O. Box 1492
   Washington, DC 20013
   800-695-0285
   202-884-8200
   www.nichcy.org

Web sites

Articles about divorce
   www.divorceonline.com

The Child Psychologist (a site for children with special needs)
   www.childpsychologist.com

Council for Children with Behavioral Disorders
   www.ccbd.net

Directory of Prescription Drug Assistance Programs
   www.phrma.org

Divorce Source—legal resource
   www.divorcesource.com

A Guide to the Individualized Education Program
   www.ed.gov/offices/OSERS/OSEP/Products/EP_Guide/

National Institute for Mental Health
   www.nimh.nih.gov

Office of the Surgeon General
   www.surgeongeneral.gov

Positive Behavioral Interventions and Supports
   www.pbis.org

Therapist Locator and childhood disorder resource
   www.4therapy.com

References

American Psychiatric Association. 2000. *Diagnostic and Statistical Manual of Mental Disorders.* 4th ed. Text Revision. Washington, D.C.: American Psychiatric Association.

Ashton, Joyce, and Dennis Ashton. 1996. *Loss and Grief Recovery.* Amityville, New York: Baywood Publishing Co., Inc.

Barkley, Russell A. 1996a. 18 ways to make token systems more effective for ADHD children and teens. *The ADHD Report* 4(4):1-5.

———. 1996b. *Hyperactive Children: A Handbook for Diagnosis and Treatment.* New York: Guilford Press.

Barton, Stuart, ed. 2001. *Clinical Evidence.* London, England: BMJ Publishing Group.

Beck, Aaron T. 1976. *Cognitive Therapy and the Emotional Disorders.* New York: International Universities Press.

Beck, Aaron T., et al. 1979. *Cognitive Therapy of Depression.* New York: Guilford Press.

Becker, Wesley C. 1971. *Parents Are Teachers.* Champaign, Illinois: Research Press.

Blount, Ronald L., et al. 1984. A brief, effective method for teaching children to swallow pills. *Behavior Therapy* 15:381-387.

Burns, David D. 1990. *The Feeling Good Handbook.* New York: Plume.

Christophersen, Edward R. 1994. *Pediatric Compliance: A Guide for the Primary Care Physician.* New York: Plenum.

Christophersen, Edward R., and Susan L. Mortweet. 2002. *Parenting That Works: Building Skills That Last a Lifetime.* Washington, D.C.: APA Books.

Christophersen, Edward R., et al. 1974a. *The Home Chip System.* Kansas City, Kansas: University of Kansas Medical Center.

Christophersen, Edward R., et al. 1974b. *The Point System.* Kansas City, Kansas: University of Kansas Medical Center.

Dix, Theodore. 1991. The affective organization of parenting: Adaptive and maladaptive processes. *Psychological Bulletin* 110:3–25.

Dudley, Charma D. 1997. *Treating Depressed Children.* Oakland, California: New Harbinger Publications.

Dujovne, Vera F. 1992. Cognitive therapy with the depressed child. Unpublished dissertation.

Dujovne, Vera F., et al. 1995. Pharmacological and cognitive-behavioral approaches in the treatment of childhood depression: A review and critique. *Clinical Psychology Review* 15:89-611.

Ellis, Albert. 1962. *Reason and Emotion in Psychotherapy.* Seacaucus, New Jersey: Lyle Stuart.

Feinberg, Linda S. 1996. *Teasing: Innocent Fun or Sadistic Malice.* Far Hills, New Jersey: New Horizon Press.

4therapy.com. 2002. *How Antidepressants Work.* Pp. 1-3.

Garfinkel, Barry D., et al. 1990. *Psychiatric Disorders in Children and Adolescents.* Philadelphia: W. B. Saunders.

Glaser, K. 1968. Masked depression in children and adolescents. *Anuals of Progressive Child Psychiatry and Child Development.* 1:345-355.

Hafen, Brent Q., et al. 1996. *Mind/Body Health: The Effects of Attitudes, Emotions, and Relationships.* Boston: Allyn and Bacon Publishing.

Hall, R. Vance, and Marilyn C. Hall. 1980. *How To Use Planned Ignoring.* Lawrence, Kansas: H and H Enterprises, Inc.

Howard, Barbara J. 1996. Advising parents on discipline: What works. *Pediatrics* 98:809–815.

Jellinek, Michael S., and James B. Snyder. 1998. Depression in children and adolescents. *Pediatrics in Review* 19:255-263.

Jongsma, Arthur E., et al. 2000. *The Child Psychotherapy Treatment Planner.* New York: John Wiley and Sons.

Kansas State Department of Education, 2001. *Section 504. ADA Guidelines for Parents.* Topeka, Kansas: Kansas State Department of Education.

Kastelic, Elizabeth A., et al. 2000. Selective serotonin reuptake inhibitors for children and adolescents. *Current Psychiatry Reports* 2:117-123.

Kutcher, Stan. 2000. Practical clinical issues regarding child and adolescent psychopharmacology. *Child and Adolescent Psychiatric Clinics of North America* 9:245-259.

Ludwig, Stephen, and Anthony Rostain. 1999. Family Function and Dysfunction. In *Developmental Behavioral Pediatrics*, edited by Melvin D. Levine, William B. Carey, and Allen C. Crocker. Philadelphia: W. B. Saunders Company.

National Information Center for Children and Youth with Disabilities. 1999a. *Individualized Education Programs.* 4th ed. Washington, D.C.: National Information Center for Children and Youth with Disabilities.

National Information Center for Children and Youth with Disabilities. 1999b. *Questions Often Asked by Parents about Special Education Services.* 4th ed. Washington, D.C.: National Information Center for Children and Youth with Disabilities.

————. 2000. *Questions and Answers about IDEA.* 2nd ed. Washington, D.C.: National Information Center for Children and Youth with Disabilities.

National Institute of Mental Health. 2002. *Depression in Children and Adolescents: A Fact Sheet for Physicians.* Bethesda, Maryland: National Institute of Mental Health.

Nelson, Eve-Lynn, et al. 2003. Treating childhood depression over interactive televideo: a randomized controlled success. *Telemedicine Journal and e-Health.*

Nurse Practitioner's Drug Handbook. 2002. Philadelphia: Lippincott, Williams, and Wilkins.

Papolos, Demitri, and Janice Papolos. 1999. *The Bipolar Child.* New York: Broadway Books.

Physician's Desk Reference. 2002. Montale, New Jersey: Medical Economics Company, Inc.

Satcher, D. 2002. Depression and Suicide in Children and Adolescents. In *Mental Health: A Report of the Surgeon General* Washington, D.C.: GPO.

Shalala, Donna E. 2001. Children and mental health. *Mental Health: A Report of the Surgeon General* Washington, D.C.: GPO.

Shoaf, Thomas L., et al. 2001. Childhood depression: Diagnosis and treatment strategies in general pediatrics. *Pediatric Annals* 30:130-137.

Tortora, Gerard J., and Sandra Reynolds Grabowski. 2000. *Human Body: The Essentials of Anatomy and Physiology.* New York: Harper-Collins.

Weiner, Jerry M., and Steven L. Jaffe. 1999. Historical Overview of Childhood and Adolescent Psychopharmacology. In *Diagnosis and Psychopharmacology of Childhood and Adolescent Disorders,* edited by Jerry M. Weiner. New York: John Wiley and Sons.

Weiten, Wayne. 1997. *Psychology: Themes and Variations.* New York: Brooks/Cole Publishing Company.

Weyburne, Darlene. 1999. *What to Tell the Kids About Your Divorce.* Oakland, CA: New Harbinger Publications.

Whalen, Carol K., and Barbara Henker. 1998. Attention-deficit/ hyperactivity disorders. In *Handbook of Child Psychopathology,* edited by T. H. Ollendick, and M. Hersen. New York: Plenum Press.

Wilens, Timothy E. 2001. *Straight Talk About Psychiatric Medications for Kids.* New York: Guilford Press.

Worden, J. William. 1991. *Grief Counseling and Grief Therapy.* New York: Springer Publishing Company.

Martha Underwood Barnard, Ph.D., is a pediatric psychologist at the KU Children's Center of the University of Kansas Medical Center, and a faculty member in the Department of Pediatrics in the Pediatric and Behavioral Sciences section at the University of Kansas and the University of Kansas Medical Center. She also holds joint appointments in the Department of Psychiatry, School of Nursing and an adjunct appointment in the Department of Psychology. She has an extensive clinical practice, where she works with children and their families in the inpatient and outpatient environments. She has written and presented local and national lectures on topics such as behavioral problems, childhood depression, childhood anxiety disorders, noncompliance to medical regimens, chronic illness, grief, palliative care, and post-traumatic stress disorder and has been active in community and national boards and programs, including a school board, state White House Conference committee, a National Commission on expanded roles in nursing, Ronald McDonald Board, and the National Academy of Practice.

With over thirty years of experience working with children and families, she has done research on noncompliance issues in health care, childhood depression, childhood chronic illness, and palliative care in children. Barnard has contributed greatly to educating the public on PTSD, self-esteem, grief, childhood depression, and youth suicide through local, national, and international interviews on radio and TV talk shows and lectures. Her previous books include *Comprehensive Pediatric Nursing* and *Family Health Nursing* in addition to numerous journal publications.

Some Other
New Harbinger Titles

The Stop Walking on Eggshells Workbook, Item SWEW $18.95

Conquer Your Critical Inner Voice, Item CYIC $15.95

The PTSD Workbook, Item PWK $17.95

Hypnotize Yourself Out of Pain Now!, Item HYOP $14.95

The Depression Workbook, 2nd edition, Item DWR2 $19.95

Beating the Senior Blues, Item YCBS $17.95

Shared Confinement, Item SDCF $15.95

Handbook of Clinical Psychopharmacology for Therpists, 3rd edition, Item HCP3 $55.95

Getting Your Life Back Together When You Have Schizophrenia Item GYLB $14.95

Do-It-Yourself Eye Movement Technique for Emotional Healing, Item DIYE $13.95

Stop the Anger Now, Item SAGN $17.95

The Self-Esteem Workbook, Item SEWB $18.95

The Habit Change Workbook, Item HBCW $19.95

The Memory Workbook, Item MMWB $18.95

The Anxiety & Phobia Workbook, 3rd edition, Item PHO3 $19.95

Beyond Anxiety & Phobia, Item BYAP $19.95

Stop Walking on Eggshells, Item WOE $15.95

The Healing Sorrow Workbook, Item HSW $17.95

The Relaxation & Stress Reduction Workbook, 5th edition, Item RS5 $19.95

Stop Controlling Me!, Item SCM $13.95

The Anger Control Workbook, Item ACWB $17.95

Call **toll free, 1-800-748-6273,** or log on to our online bookstore at **www.newharbinger.com** to order. Have your Visa or Mastercard number ready. Or send a check for the titles you want to New Harbinger Publications, Inc., 5674 Shattuck Ave., Oakland, CA 94609. Include $4.50 for the first book and 75¢ for each additional book, to cover shipping and handling. (California residents please include appropriate sales tax.) Allow two to five weeks for delivery.

Prices subject to change without notice.